DELIVER US
FROM EVIL

A Guide to Spiritual Warfare

For
Thomas, Peter & Andrew

Table of Contents

Illustration for John Milton's "Paradise Lost" by Gustave Doré, 1866

WHO IS THE DEVIL?

[8]Again, the devil took him to a very high mountain and showed him all the kingdoms of the world and their splendor. [9]"All this I will give you," he said, "if you will bow down and worship me."
[10]Jesus said to him, "Away from me, Satan! For it is written: 'Worship the Lord your God, and serve him only.'"
[11]Then the devil left him, and angels came and attended him.
Matthew 4:8-11

Christianity

Christianity teaches that Satan was once an angel called Lucifer, who, in love with his own beauty, fell into pride and self-centeredness. Lucifer" means "Light-Bringer" or "Day Star." Ezekiel calls him "the anointed cherub"" which means he was one of the chief angels in heaven. He is specifically shown to be a created being, possibly the most beautiful, wise, and perfect of God's creations. But Lucifer grew proud and vain in his beauty. He began to become envious of God's power over the universe, and over maybe millions of years, he schemed to induce other angels to support him in an attempt to overthrow God. When he finally led one third of the angels to war against God in heaven, God cast him and his angelic troops back to the earth (Luke 10:18 And he said unto them, I beheld Satan as lightning fall from heaven.) Satan has three main goals: He wants control, he wants to determine your destiny, and he wants to steal the life that God gave you, and when he is through with it, he will only destroy it. To accomplish this he may do things like destroy your confidence or your good character. He may try to cause you confusion about your faith. Getting people to doubt the scriptures has been his primary attack.

Catholicism

Catholics believe that the devil and other demons were angels created by God who became demonic, or adversaries of God, after their fall. Satan, lord of demons, exists and can cause humans harm, but he is still a creature and not equal to God.

Hinduism

Though Hindus believe there is evil in the world, there is no single devil-like entity in Hinduism. However, there is a concept of *asura,* or evil sprit. Evil spirits do not remain evil forever--they are beings of *Naraka,* the lower plane, and can evolve to goodness. The Bhagavad Gita, one of Hinduism's most important texts, tells the story of Arjuna's fight against evil and lower desires, embodied by the army of Kauravas.

Buddhism

The Buddhist concept of the devil is called Mara, the head of the heavenly demons and the Sense Desire realm. Buddhists believe that Siddhartha was tempted by Mara before enlightenment, but he could not be swayed from his path. Mara symbolizes desire and everything that hinders humans from proceeding along the right path.

Islam

Iblis, the devil in Islam, is described in the Qur'an as "the adversary." Originally, he refused to obey God's commandment to prostrate himself before Adam. The devil in Islam tempts humans and tries to mislead them. Before beginning to read the Qur'an, Muslims recite the *Ta'awud,* in which they say, "I take refuge in God from Satan the stoned one"--praying that they may take refuge in Allah from the devil.

Judaism

Judaism teaches that humans were created with two inclinations, the *yetzer tov,* or good inclination, and the *yetzer ra,* the bad inclination. The inclination to do bad or be selfish is within a person, it is not the result of an outside force. The Jewish concept of Satan, the "hinderer," is that he is an angel who leads humans to evil, and people must struggle to overcome their evil inclinations.

Wicca

Wiccans do not have a concept of the devil in their beliefs or practices. Wiccans do not believe that good and evil come from a divine source, but instead individual humans are responsible for their actions.

Illustration for John Milton's "Paradise Lost" by Gustave Doré, 1866.

Ephesians 6:11

FAITH

THE ARMOR OF GOD

"Put on the whole armor of God that you may be able to stand against the wiles of the devil"- Eph 6:11

The wearing of medieval armor was an effective means of protection in war and combat for centuries. The object of medieval armor was to protect the wearer from attack from the most powerful weapons of the period. Armor use dates back to the Greek and early Roman Empire. Medieval era knights are most remembered for their

11

elaborate armor. A knight's armor was more than protection; it reflected his status and lifestyle. The quality of the armor was as important as the overall look and the battle efficiency.

Your spiritual armor works to project you in a spiritual war against evil and Satan. The more powerful your faith and the more you arm yourself with the armor of God, the easier it is for you to defend yourself against forces of evil. The bible uses the analogy of armor for the purpose of protection in battle to putting on the armor of God as protection against the evils that we face every day. With the knowledge that we are wearing the armor of God, we feel that we have added strength and are able to persevere against the wiles of Satan and strongly stand on the side of the righteous.

Ephesians 6:10-18

[10] Finally, my brethren, be strong in the Lord, and in the power of his might. [11] Put on the whole armor of God, that you may be able to stand against the wiles of the devil. [12] For we wrestle not against flesh and blood, but against principalities, against powers, against the rulers of the darkness of this world, against spiritual wickedness in high places. [13] Wherefore take unto you the whole armor of God, that you may be able to withstand in the evil day, and having done all, to stand. [14] Stand therefore, having your loins girt about with truth, and having on the breastplate of righteousness; [15] And your feet shod with the preparation of the gospel of peace; [16] Above all, taking the shield of faith, wherewith you shall be able to quench all the fiery darts of the wicked. [17] And take the helmet of salvation, and the sword of the Spirit, which is the word of God: [18] Praying always with all prayer and supplication in the Spirit, and watching thereunto with all perseverance and supplication for all saints.

Prayer to put on the Armor of God

Lord God I am putting on your armor to protect me from the evil one. I'm putting on the Helmet of Salvation to protect my mind from evil or negative thoughts or feelings, but Lord God I'm also adding the Blinders to protect my eyes from sin. Lord God I want to stay on your straight and narrow path. I do not what to look Left or Right where there could be sin. And if sin comes directly in front of me Lord God, let my eyes look away. Lord God I am putting on the Chest plate of righteousness to protect my heart, my soul and the rest of my organs from evil or negative thoughts, feelings or actions. Lord God I'm fastening the Belt of Truth around my waist so I know when the truth is being told to me or if it is a lie from Satan. I myself will tell the truth. Lord God I am putting on the footgear so that I will be able to spread the Great Gospel of Peace. Lord God I carry the Shield of Faith for when Satan shoots his flaming arrows at me, they will be extinguished and be of no harm to me. And Lord God I carry the Sword of the Holy Spirit, the Word of God, for nothing can defeat it for the Word of God is the absolute truth

-   Amen

Albrecht Dürer 1513 The Knight, Death and Devil

14

St. Michael's fight against the dragon 1498 Dürer, Albrecht

SAINT MICHAEL THE ARCHANGEL

"And there was war in heaven: Michael and his angels fought against the dragon; and the dragon fought and his angels, And prevailed not; neither was their place found any more in heaven. And the great dragon was cast out, that old serpent, called the Devil, and Satan, which deceives the whole world: he was cast out into the earth, and his angels were cast out with him." Rev 12:7-9

Michael is the leader of the angels who remained faithful to God during the Great War of Heaven, when Lucifer strove against his Creator. As the leader of the angelic hosts, he overcame Lucifer and his followers and cast them out of heaven. "And there was a great battle in heaven, Michael and his angels fought with the dragon." St. John speaks of the great conflict at the end of time, the Apocalypse, which is a reflection of that first great battle. Holy Scripture describes St. Michael as "one of the chief princes," and leader of the forces of heaven in their triumph over the powers of hell. As St. Michael is often depicted as taming (or slaying) an evil being, he is a wonderful Archangel to call upon when we need help taming the evils within our lives.

Pope Leo XIII and St. Michael

This is how this prayer came to be written: It is said that one day having celebrated the Holy Sacrifice, the aged Pontiff Leo XIII was in conference with the Cardinals. Suddenly he sank to the floor in a deep swoon. Physicians who hastened to his side feared that he had already expired, for they could find no trace of his pulse. However, after a short interval the Holy Father rallied, and opening his eyes exclaimed with great emotion: "Oh what a horrible picture I was permitted to see!" He had been shown in spirit the tremendous activities of the evil spirits and their ravings against the Church. But in the midst of this vision of horror he had also beheld consoling visions of the glorious Archangel Michael, who had appeared and cast Satan and his legions back into the abyss of hell. Soon afterward he composed the well-known prayer to the Archangel. This is the original version of the prayer to St Michael as written by Pope Leo XIII. It is taken from The Raccolta, twelfth edition, published by Burnes, Oates & Washbourne Ltd. It was originally published in the Roman Raccolta of July 23, 1898, and in a supplement approved July 31, 1902.

Pope Leo XIII c. 1898

The Raccolta is a book containing, arranged in convenient order, the prayers, novenas, pious practices, etc. to which general indulgences have been attached, as well as the decrees and rescripts granting the indulgences, and the conditions requisite for gaining them. All the indulgences contained the Raccolta are applicable to the souls in purgatory. The Raccolta was first published at Rome in 1807. It is forbidden to publish a translation of the entire Raccolta without the approval of the Roman congregation There is one approved edition of the Raccolta in English, especially adapted for the use of the faithful. The full title of the last official edition is: *"Raccolta di orazioni e pie opere, per le quali sono state concesse dai Sommi Pontefici le SS. Indulgenze"* (Rome, 1898).

Original Prayer to St. Michael

O Glorious Archangel St. Michael, Prince of the heavenly host, be our defense in the terrible warfare, which we carry on against principalities and powers, against the rulers of this world of darkness, spirits of evil. Come to the aid of man, whom God created immortal, made in His own image and likeness, and redeemed at a great price from the tyranny of the devil.

Fight this day the battle of the Lord, together with the holy angels, as already thou hast fought the leader of the proud angels, Lucifer, and his apostate host, who were powerless to resist thee, nor was there place for them any longer in heaven. That cruel, that ancient serpent, who is called the devil or Satan who seduces the whole world, was cast into the abyss with his angels. Behold, this primeval enemy and slayer of men has taken courage.

Transformed into an angel of light, he wanders about with all the multitude of wicked spirits, invading the earth in order to blot out the name of God and of His Christ, to seize upon, slay and cast into eternal perdition souls destined for the crown of eternal glory. This wicked dragon pours out, as a most impure flood, the venom of his malice on men of depraved mind and corrupt heart, the spirit of lying, of impiety, of blasphemy, and the pestilent breath of impurity, and of every vice and iniquity.

These most crafty enemies have filled and inebriated with gall and bitterness the Church, the spouse of the immaculate Lamb, and have laid impious hands on her most sacred possessions. In the Holy Place itself, where has been set up the See of the most holy Peter and the Chair of Truth for the light of the world, they have raised the throne of their abominable impiety, with the iniquitous design that when the Pastor has been struck, the sheep may be scattered.

Arise then, O invincible Prince, bring help against the attacks of the lost spirits to the people of God, and give them the victory. They venerate thee as their protector and patron; in thee holy Church glories as her defense against the malicious power of hell; to thee has God entrusted the souls of men to be established in heavenly beatitude. Oh, pray to the God of peace that He may put Satan under our feet, so far conquered that he may no longer be able to hold men in captivity and harm the Church. Offer our prayers in the sight of the Most High, so that they may quickly conciliate the mercies of the Lord; and beating down the dragon, the ancient serpent, who is the devil and Satan, do thou again make him captive in the abyss, that he may no longer seduce the nations.

Amen.

Verse: Behold the Cross of the Lord; be scattered ye hostile powers.
Response: The Lion of the tribe of Juda has conquered the root of David.
Verse: Let Thy mercies be upon us, O Lord.
Response: As we have hoped in Thee.
Verse: O Lord, hear my prayer.
Response: And let my cry come unto Thee.

Let us pray.

O God, the Father of our Lord Jesus Christ, we call upon Thy holy name, and as supplicants we implore Thy clemency, that by the intercession of Mary, ever Virgin immaculate and our Mother, and of the glorious Archangel St. Michael, Thou wouldst deign to help us against Satan and all other unclean spirits, who wander about the world for the injury of the human race and the ruin of souls.

Amen.

The following prayer is from the Raccolta of May 1934.

First Part of the Glorious St. Michael's Exorcism

O glorious Prince of the heavenly host, St. Michael, the Archangel, defend us in the battle and in the fearful warfare that we are waging against the principalities and powers, against the rulers of this world of darkness, against the evil spirits. Come thou to the assistance of men, whom Almighty God created immortal, making them in His own image and likeness and redeeming them at a great price from the tyranny of Satan.

Fight this day the battle of the Lord with thy legions of holy Angels, even as of old thou didst fight against Lucifer, the leader of the proud spirits and all his rebel angels, who were powerless to stand against thee, neither was their place found any more in heaven. And that apostate angel, transformed into an angel of darkness who still creeps about the earth to encompass our ruin, was cast headlong into the abyss together with his followers. But behold, that first enemy of mankind, and a murderer from the beginning, has regained his confidence. Changing himself into an angel of light, he goes about with the whole multitude of the wicked spirits to invade the earth and blot out the name of God and of His Christ, to plunder, to slay and to consign to eternal damnation the souls that have been destined for a crown of everlasting life.

This wicked serpent, like an unclean torrent, pours into men of depraved minds and corrupt hearts the poison of his malice, the spirit of lying, impiety and blasphemy, and the deadly breath of impurity and every form of vice and iniquity. These crafty enemies of mankind have filled to overflowing with gall and wormwood the Church, which is the Bride of the lamb without spot; they have laid profane hands upon her most sacred treasures. Make haste, therefore, O invincible Prince, to help the people of God against the inroads of the lost spirits and grant us the victory. Amen.

Photo by Anne Palagruto

Short Prayer to St. Michael

Saint Michael the Archangel, defend us in battle, be our protection against the wickedness and snares of the devil; may God rebuke him we humbly pray; and do thou, O Prince of the Heavenly host, by the power of God, thrust into hell Satan and all evil spirits who wander through the world for the ruin of souls. Amen.

Latin Version
Sancte Míchael Archángele, defénde nos in proélio contra nequítiam et insídias diáboli esto præsídium. Imperet illi Deus, súpplices deprecámur: tuque, princeps milítiæ cæléstis, Sátanam aliósque spíritus malígnos, qui ad perditiónem animárum pervagántur in mundo, divína virtúte, In inférnum detrude. Amen

St. Michael and dragon   Raphael

Act of Consecration to St. Michael

Oh most Noble Prince of the Angelic Hierarchies valorous warrior of Almighty God, and zealous lover of his glory, terror of the rebellious angels, and love and delight of all the just ones, my beloved Archangel Saint Michael, desiring to be numbered among your devoted servants, I, today offer and consecrate myself to you, and place myself, my family, and all I possess under your most powerful protection. I entreat you not to look at how little, I, as your servant have to offer, being only a wretched sinner, but to gaze, rather, with favorable eye at the heartfelt affection with which this offering is made, and remember that if from this day onward I am under your patronage, you must during all my life assist me, and procure for me the pardon of my many grievous offenses, and sins, the grace to love with all my heart my God, my dear Savior

Jesus, and my Sweet Mother Mary, and obtain for me all the help necessary to arrive to my crown of glory. Defend me always from my spiritual enemies, particularly in the last moments of my life. Come then oh Glorious Prince and succor me in my last struggle, and with your powerful weapon cast far from me into the infernal abyss that prevaricator and proud angel that one day you prostrated in the celestial battle. Saint Michael defend us in our daily battle so that we may not perish in the last Judgment.

HEDGE PYAYERS

"The angel of the Lord encamps around those who fear Him, and rescues them." —Psalm 34:7

The "Hedge Prayer for Protection" is one of the most powerful prayers in the arsenal of spiritual warfare. We learn from Job that God has placed a "hedge of protection" around his children that Satan cannot cross (James 4:7-8) except that God allows it (or as we allow it). It should be noted, as it is with all prayer, the Hedge Prayer of Protection is not a magic bullet. There are no guarantees that the Hedge surrounding us cannot be breached. We can allow Satan and his demons to breach the Hedge by our carelessness of leaving the gate open, through direct or indirect invitation to the demons.

Hedge Prayer for Protection of Self

Trusting in the promise that whatever we ask the Father in Jesus' name He will do, I now approach You Our Father with confidence in Our Lord's words and in Your infinite power and love for me, and with the intercession of the Blessed Virgin Mary, Mother of God, the Blessed Apostles Peter and Paul, Blessed Archangel Michael, my guardian angel, with all the saints and angels of heaven, and Holy in the power of His blessed Name, as ask you Father to protect me and keep me from the harassment of the devil and his minions. Father I ask that You build a hedge of protection around me, like that which surrounded Job, and to help me to keep that hedge repaired and the gate locked so that the devil and his minions have no access or means to breach the hedge except by your expressed will. Father, I know that I am powerless against the spiritual forces of evil and recognize my utter dependence on You and Your power. Look with mercy upon me. Do not look upon my sins, O Lord; rather, look at the sufferings of your Beloved Son and see the Victim who's bitter passion and death has reconciled us to You. By the victory of the cross, protect me from all evil and rebuke any evil spirits who wish to attack, influence, or breach Your hedge of protection in any way. Send them back to Hell and fortify Your Hedge for my protection by the blood of Your Son, Jesus. Send your Holy Angels to watch over me and protect me. Father, all of these things I ask in the most holy name of Jesus Christ, Your Son. Thank you, Father, for hearing my prayer. I love You, I worship You, I thank You and I trust in You.
Amen.

Ángel de la Guarda   18th century

Hedge Prayer for Protection of Others

Trusting in the promise that whatever we ask the Father in Jesus' name He will do, I now approach You Father with confidence in Our Lord's words and in Your infinite power and love for me and for *[name]*, and with the intercession of the Blessed Virgin Mary, Mother of God, the Blessed Apostles Peter and Paul, Blessed Archangel Michael, my guardian angel and the guardian angels of *[name*, with all the saints and angels of heaven, and Holy in the power of His blessed Name, as ask you Father to protect *[name]* and keep him from the harassment of the devil and his minions. Father I ask on behalf of *[name]* that You build a hedge of protection around him, like that which surrounded Job, and to help *[name]* to keep that hedge repaired and the gate locked so that the devil and his minions have no access or means to breach the hedge except by your expressed will. Father, I know that we are powerless against the spiritual forces of evil and recognize our utter dependence on You and Your power. Look with mercy upon *[name]* . Do not look upon his sins, O Lord; rather, look at the sufferings of your Beloved Son and see the Victim whose bitter passion and death has reconciled us to You. By the victory of the cross, **protect (*[name]*** from all evil and rebuke any evil spirits who wish to attack, influence, or breach Your hedge of protection in any way. Send them back to Hell and fortify Your Hedge for his protection by the blood of Your Son, Jesus. Send your Holy Angels to watch over him and protect him. Father, all of these things I ask in the most holy name of Jesus Christ, Your Son. Thank you, Father, for hearing my prayer. I love You, I worship You, I thank You and I trust in You. Amen.

Satan before the Lord   Corrado Giaguinto 1750

PRAYERS AGAINST EVIL

"Courage is fear that has said its prayers."
-    Dorothy Bernard

Prayer to Defeat the Work of Satan

O Divine Eternal Father, in union with Your Divine Son and
the Holy Spirit, and through the Immaculate Heart of Mary, I
beg You to destroy the power of Your greatest enemy - the evil
spirits Cast them into the deepest recesses of hell and chain
them there forever! Take possession of Your Kingdom which
You have created and which is rightfully Yours, Heavenly
Father, give us the reign of the Sacred Heart of Jesus and the

Immaculate Heart of Mary. I repeat this prayer out of pure love for You with every beat of my heart and with every breath I take. August Queen of Heaven! Sovereign Mistress of the angels! You who from the beginning have received from God the power and mission to crush the head of Satan, we humbly beseech you to send your holy Legions, that, under your command and by your power, they may pursue the evil spirits, encounter them on every side, resist their bold attacks and drive them hence into the abyss of eternal woe. Amen.

Temptation and Fall from the Sistine Chapel Ceiling

Prayer against demonic snares

Lord Jesus Christ, the Son of God, having struck down the ancient serpent and bound him in Tartarus by bonds of darkness, protect me from his snares. Through the prayers of our Most Holy Lady, the Theotokos and Ever-virgin Mary, of the holy Archangel Michael and all the Heavenly hosts, of the holy Prophet and Baptist John, of the holy Evangelist John the Theologian, of the holy Martyr Cyprian and the Martyr Justinia, of St. Nicholas the wonderworker, of St. Nikita of Novgorod, of St. John of Shanghai and San Francisco, the wonderworker ... and of all the saints, by the power of the life-giving Cross and by the intercession of my Guardian Angel, deliver me from evil spirits, from cunning people, from sorcery, curses, the evil eye, and from any slanders of the enemy. By Thine almighty power preserve me from evil, so that I, enlightened by Thy light, may safely reach the quiet anchorage of the Heavenly Kingdom and there eternally thank Thee, my Savior, together with Thine unoriginate Father and Thy Most Holy and Life-giving Spirit. Amen.

Prayer Against Every Evil

Spirit Of Our God, Father, Son , And Holy Spirit, Most Holy Trinity, Immaculate Virgin Mary, Angles, Archangels, And Saints Of Heaven, Descend Upon Us. Please Purify Us, Lord, Mold Us, Fill Us With Yourself, Use Us. Banish All The Forces Of Evil From Us, Destroy Them, Vanquish Them, So That We Can Be Healthy And Do Good Deeds. Banish From Us All Spells, Witchcraft, Black Magic, Malefice, Ties, Maledictions, And The Evil Eye; Diabolic Infestations, Oppressions, Possessions; All That Is Evil And Sinful, Jealousy, Perfidy, Envy; Physical, Psychological, Moral, Spiritual, Diabolical Ailments. Burn All These Evils In Hell, That They May Never Again Touch Me Or Any Other Creature In The Entire World. I

Command And Bid All The Powers Who Molest Me -- By The Power Of God All Powerful, In The Name Of Jesus Christ Our Savior, Through The Intercession Of The Immaculate Virgin Mary -- To Leave Us Forever, And To Be Consigned Into The Everlasting Hell, Where They Will Be Bound By Saint Michael The Archangel, Saint Gabriel, Saint Raphael, our guardian angels, and where they will be crushed under the heel of the Immaculate Virgin Mary.

Prayer by a Priest for a Home Bothered by Evil Spirits

O Lord God of our salvation, Son of the Living God, Who is borne by the Cherubim, being above all dominions, principalities, authorities and powers: You are great and fearsome to all around You. You are the One Who set the heavens like a vault and made the earth in Your might; Who directs the universe in Your wisdom. When earthquakes occur under heaven from the foundations, its pillars are unshaken. You speak and the sun does not shine. You sealed the stars. You forbad the seas and dried them up. Authorities and dominions hide from Your wrath, and the rock trembles before You. You obliterated the gates of brass and demolished the bars of iron. You bound the Mighty One and smashed his vessels. By Your Cross You cast down tyrants and drew in the Serpent with the hook of Your humanity. Having cast him down, You bound him with hooks in the gloom of Tartarus.

As the same Lord, the Hope of those who place their confirmation on You, and the Wall of might for those whose expectation is in You, anathematize, drive away and transform all diabolical actions and all satanic indictments, all slanders of the Adversary, and of the powers lying under this roof. Free those bearing the Sign which is awesome against demons: the Cross of Your victory, and calling upon Your gracious Name, from possession by him and from those wandering about under this roof.

Yea, Lord, You drove away legions of demons, and the demons and unclean spirits by which the deaf and dumb were held. These You commanded to depart and not to return again. You have consumed all the armies of our invisible enemies, and have made wise the faithful who have known You. For You said, "Behold, I give you power to trample underfoot snakes and scorpions, and all the power of enemies" (Luke 10:19).

Preserve, O Master, all who live in the house from all harm and every temptation from below, delivering them from fear of the feeble one and the arrows that fly by day, from things proceeding from the darkness and attacks by demons at midday. Let Your servants and Your children, delighting in Your help, and preserved by armies of angels, faithfully sing with one accord: "The Lord is my Helper and I will not be afraid; what can man do to me?" and again, "I will fear no evil, for You are with me." As You are my Confirmation, O God, Mighty Master, Prince of Peace, and Father of the age to come, for Your kingdom is an eternal Kingdom, to you alone is the Kingdom, and the Power, and the Glory, with the Father and the Holy Spirit, now and ever and unto ages of ages. Amen.

Prayer to Bind the Enemy

Heavenly Father, we come before You, trusting in Christ's payment for us and we ask that You would bind and gag all evil spirits and forces of darkness in, near and around us, so that they may not interfere with us now. We acknowledge that You are the Ruler "Far above all principality and power and might and dominion, and every name that is named, not only in this age but also in that which is to come." You have told us, in Your faithfulness, "I will give you the keys of the kingdom of heaven; whatever you bind on earth will be bound in heaven, and whatever you loose on earth will be loosed in heaven." We claim our position with You, through Your Grace and ask that as it is written, so it be done. In the Name of the Lord Jesus Christ we ask and in faith we receive. Amen.

Prayer for Breaking Satanic Covenants

I renounce ever signing my name over to Satan or having my name signed over to Satan. I announce that my name is written in the Lamb's Book of Life. I renounce any ceremony where I may have been wed to Satan, and I announce that I am the Bride of Christ. I renounce all satanic assignments, covenants; pacts and dedications that I made with Satan, or that were made for me. I announce that I am a partaker of the new covenant with Christ. I reject and renounce all curses and assignments made for me or by me for the service of Satan. (Stop here and renounce any specific pacts remembered.) I trust only in the shed Blood of my Lord, Jesus Christ and what He accomplished on the cross. I look to the Holy

Spirit for guidance. I renounce all guardians and surrogate parents assigned to me by Satanists. I renounce all baptisms, rituals or teachings by Satanists. I announce that I have been baptized into Christ Jesus and my identity is now in Christ. I renounce and reject all demons and familiar spirits attached to any part of me, by Satanists. I reject all spirit guides assigned to me. I announce that God is my Heavenly Father and the Holy Spirit is my guardian. By this, I am sealed until the day of my redemption. I will accept only God's assignment for me. In Jesus name.

Amen.

Prayer for Protection - Guardian Angels

Heavenly Father, You have sent angels to relay Your messages to us, to protect us from danger, and to rescue us from the Evil One. I thank You for the precious gift of these holy guardians that You assigned to me and my loved ones. O Lord, give us Your help through our angels to fend off the evil spirits that tempt us, that send us deceptive messages, that try to cause divisions, and all others who seek the ruin of our souls. I also pray that the guardian angels of my church, my town and my nation will have all the strength and power they need to protect us from the snares and attacks of wickedness. Guardian angels, pray for us.

Amen

Battle Against Evil - Prayer to St. Theodore Tyro

O Heavenly King, Saint Theodore was a young soldier in the Roman army when he converted to Christianity. Though he was ordered to fight enemies of the empire, he believed that the devil was the only true enemy. Soon, he was killed for being a Christian, thus winning the battle against the demons who wanted to keep him out of Heaven. I ask him to pray for my fight against evil and temptation and to pray for all my loved ones during their battles. Help us, O victorious Jesus, to turn away from sin and to grow in holiness. Teach us how to always wear the armor of God. Saint Theodore, pray for us.

Amen.

Overcoming Evil - Prayer to St. Wolfgang

Blessed Redeemer, Saint Wolfgang was a monk and a bishop who had the gifts of teaching and healing. He evangelized the pagan empire of his country's enemy in order to reduce the threat of attack. Legend says that he forced Satan to help him build a church. I ask him to pray for our celebration of All Hallow's Eve, that it be converted from a glorification of the occult into a preparation for honoring the saints. Help us to build up the Communion of Saints. Teach us to evangelize those who are fascinated with fear, evil, and death. Dear Jesus, fill them with Your love, Your grace, and Your holiness. Saint Wolfgang, pray for us.

Amen.

St. Benedict of Nursia 1926 by Herman Nieg

Prayer for Protection - St. Benedict

Good Jesus, Saint Benedict believed in excelling and doing his very best to honor You. When he attended school, the undisciplined attitude of the other students dismayed him. Later, when he founded twelve monasteries, the demand for spiritual excellence in his Monastic Rule was so frustrating to lazy monks, some of them tried to poison him, but he blessed the drink and consumed it with no ill effects. I ask him to pray for the protection of my family, my church, and my friendships against the wickedness of Satan. Teach us, O Lord, to use Your cross to conquer the evil in our world today. Saint Benedict, pray for us. Amen.

St. George   Raffaello Sanzio C. 1490

Prayer for Victory - St. George

Mighty God, Saint George was nicknamed the "Victory Bringer" because he relied on Your power to defeat evil wherever he went. Starting out as a soldier in his country's army, he converted and became a soldier for

Christ. Laying down the world's armor by giving his wealth to the poor, he forever after carried the shield of faith and won many victories for those who sought Your help. I ask him to pray for the battles I've been enduring, and to bring Your triumph into my life. Help me to overcome the Enemy, Lord Jesus, and teach me how to protect myself with ever-increasing faith. Saint George, pray for me. Amen.

Prayer For Deliverance

My Lord, You are all powerful, You are God, you are Father. We beg you through the intercession and help of the archangels Michael, Raphael, and Gabriel, for the deliverance of our brothers and sisters who are enslaved by the evil one. All saints of heaven, come to our aid. From anxiety, sadness, and obsessions, We beg You. *Free us, O Lord*. From hatred, fornication, envy, We beg You. *Free us, O Lord*. From thoughts of jealousy, rage, and death. We beg You. *Free us, O Lord*. From every thought of suicide and abortion. We beg You. From the onslaught of this sniper, we beg You: *Free us, O Lord*. From every form of sinful sexuality. We beg You. *Free us, O Lord*. From every division in our family, and every harmful friendship. We beg You. *Free us, O Lord*. From every sort of spell, malefice, witchcraft, and every form of the occult and homicide. We beg You. *Free us, O Lord*.
Lord, You who said, "I leave you peace, my peace I give you," grant that, through the intercession of the Virgin Mary, we may be liberated from every evil spell and enjoy Your peace always. In the name of Christ, our Lord. *Amen.*

Renunciation of Satan

Satan,
I renounce you and all your works, including all and whatsoever witchcraft, voodoo, spiritism, tarot cards, everything that directly or disguised might have any connection with you. I also renounce now whatsoever connection that I or members of my family, friends and acquaintances may have had with your works.

I renounce you, satan, in the name of Jesus Christ and I order you to leave me now, in the name of Jesus Christ, the Son of the living God, my savior. Amen."

Renunciation Of Satan and Claiming the Full Victory
From the
Order of the Legion of St. Michael

I claim the full victory that my Lord Jesus Christ won on the Cross for me. Having disarmed the powers and authorities, He made a public spectacle of them, triumphing over them by the cross" (Col. 2:15) His victory for me is my victory.

In the name of the Lord Jesus Christ I renounce all the workings of Satan in my life in all its forms, whether brought into my life by my actions or by others. I break all attachments, ground, curses, spells, and rights Satan may have in my life whether such ground was gained through my actions or through others. Strengthened by the intercession of the Immaculate Virgin Mary, Mother of God, of Blessed Michael the Archangel, of the Blessed

Apostles Peter and Paul, and all the Saints and Angels of Heaven, and powerful in the holy authority of the name of the Lord Jesus Christ, I ask you Lord to command Satan and all his minions, whomever they may be, to get out of my life and stay out. With that authority I now take back the ground in my life gained by Satan through my sins. I reclaim this ground and my life for Christ. I now dedicate myself to the Lord Jesus Christ; I belong to Him alone. Amen.

Resisting Satan's Attack Against Our Household

In the name of the Lord Jesus Christ, strengthened by the intercession of the Immaculate Virgin Mary, Mother of God, of Blessed Michael the Archangel, of the Blessed Apostles Peter and Paul, and all the Saints and Angels of Heaven, and powerful in the holy authority of His name, *and by my authority as head of the household,* I(we) come before You Heavenly Father to ask you to come against the powers of darkness causing *(name whatever symptom)*. Come against these powers, O Lord, because of the power of my(our) union with the Lord Jesus Christ. According to Your Word, O Lord, and through His precious blood I(we) resist the devil and his minions. I(we) resist the devil and all of his workers by the Person and power of the Lord Jesus Christ. I(we) submit *(and submit this household)* to the Lordship and control of the Lord Jesus, and I(we) as you Father to bring the power of my(our) Lord's incarnation, His crucifixion, His resurrection, His ascension, His glorification, and His second coming directly to focus against all evil forces and all of the evil work against _____. *(By the authority of my position as head of the household),* I(we) claim my(our) union with the Lord Jesus Christ, and I(we) resist the devil; I(we) resist the devil and all his minions, and I(we) ask You heavenly Father to force these evil ones to flee from before the truth of God.

Further, O Lord, I (we) ask You to bind together the whole kingdom of the evil one and to bind them from working, and finally to command all evil forces and their kingdom to leave _____ and to go where the Lord Jesus Christ may sends them. Amen.

Prayer for Breaking Curses From Our Lives

The way to break a curse is to repent for whatever involvement has occurred on the enemy's territory and rebuke the devil out of your life. You should also pray something along the following lines:

"Father, I ask you first to forgive me for my sins and cleanse me from any area where I have allowed the devil to enter my life. I renounce any involvement with the works of darkness. In the name of Jesus, I now cancel every curse, and Father, I ask you to forgive the people who have spoken them against me. I thank you that those curses will no longer operate against me. In Jesus' name, they are broken right now, by the power of Almighty God. I cancel every evil that was spoken against me and ask you to cover me and my family with your protection according to your Word in **Psalm 91**."

Psalm 91

[1] He who dwells in the shelter of the Most High
will rest in the shadow of the Almighty.
[2] I will say of the LORD, "He is my refuge and my
fortress, my God, in whom I trust."
[3] Surely he will save you from the fowler's snare
and from the deadly pestilence.
[4] He will cover you with his feathers, and under his wings
you will find refuge; his faithfulness will be your shield
and rampart. [5] You will not fear the terror of night,
nor the arrow that flies by day,
[6] nor the pestilence that stalks in the darkness,
nor the plague that destroys at midday.
[7] A thousand may fall at your side, ten thousand at your
right hand, but it will not come near you.
[8] You will only observe with your eyes
and see the punishment of the wicked.
[9] If you make the Most High your dwelling-
even the LORD, who is my refuge-
[10] then no harm will befall you, no disaster will come near
your tent.
[11] For he will command his angels concerning you to
guard you in all your ways;
[12] they will lift you up in their hands, so that you will not
strike your foot against a stone.
[13] You will tread upon the lion and the cobra;
you will trample the great lion and the serpent.
[14] "Because he loves me," says the LORD, "I will rescue
him; I will protect him, for he acknowledges my name.
[15] He will call upon me, and I will answer him; I will be
with him in trouble, I will deliver him and honor him.
[16] With long life will I satisfy him and show him my
salvation."

Hexenszene - David Teniers C. 1863

Prayer To Be Freed From A Curse

"Lord Jesus Christ,
I believe You are the Son of God and the only way to
God, that You died on the Cross for my sins and for me
You were resurrected from the dead. I believe with what

44

You did for me as my foundation, that the vindications of satan against me have been cancelled by Your Cross. Therefore, Lord Jesus, I entrust myself to You, and I promise to serve and obey You. Because of this I oppose any malignant force of darkness that in any way has come into my life - either by my own acts, or by acts of my family or ancestors or any other thing which I was not aware of. Wherever there may be any shadows in my life, any malignant forces, I now renounce them, Lord. I refuse to submit to them any longer, and, in the mighty name of Jesus, the Son of God, I sit in judgment over all the forces of evil that torment me. I detach myself from them and absolutely free myself from their power. I call on the Holy Spirit of God to take me over, completely and absolutely, freeing me and detaching me from evil as only the Spirit of God can do. In the name of Jesus Christ. Amen."

Prayer for Protection (1)

by Kaye Johns

Holy Father, we come secure in the knowledge that we are righteous in Your sight because of Jesus' death on the cross. It is in His powerful name that we pray, the name at which every knee shall bow. We ask You to bind Satan and his evil spirits away from ourselves and these we love, in the name of Jesus and in the power of His blood, which overcomes the accuser. We ask You to send these evil spirits wherever Jesus tells them to go.
In the truth of Your Word, we come against the father of lies, asking that Jesus, the Way, the Truth and the Life,

set us free from Satan's influence. We stand against the deceiver, asking the Holy Spirit of Truth to reveal to us when Satan is trying to disguise himself as an angel of light. We come against the tempter, asking for the strength to watch and pray, to have victory over temptation through Your Word. We ask that You not allow the thief to snatch Your Word from us, for You have promised Your Word will not return void. We come against the accuser who tries to discourage us with guilt regarding sins You have already forgiven, for Jesus is our Advocate.

We stand against Satan's strongholds in our lives, and any sins that have given the devil a foothold. We ask for broken and contrite hearts, willing to confess and repent and to live in Your strength. We ask You to bring all our thoughts captive to the obedience of Christ.
We thank You that we are Your children, and Satan cannot harm us without Your permission. We have put our hope in the living God, Who is the Savior of all men -- Jesus, in Whose name we pray. *Amen.*

Prayer for Protection (2)

Eternal Father, I offer the Most Precious Blood of thy Divine Son Jesus in union with all the masses said throughout the world today for all the Holy Souls in purgatory, for sinners everywhere in the Universal Church, to those in my home and within my family, I place my self in the presence of Jesus Christ and submit to His Lordship. In the name of Jesus Christ crucified, died and risen: I bind all the spirits of the air, the atmosphere, the water, the fire, the wind, the ground, the underground and the nether world.I also bind the influence of any lost or fallen soul who may be present, and all the emissaries of the satanic headquarters or any coven of witches or warlocks or satan worshippers who may be present in some preternatural way.

I claim the blood of Jesus on the air and atmosphere, the water, the fire, the wind, the ground and their fruits all around us, the underground and the nether world.

In the Name of Jesus Christ, I forbid every adversary mentioned to communicate with or help one another in any way or to communicate with me or to do anything at all except what I command in Jesus' Name.

In the Name of Jesus Christ, I seal this place, and all present, and all family and associates of those present and their places and possessions and sources of supply in the Blood of Jesus. *(3x)*

In the Name of Jesus Christ, I forbid any lost spirits, covens, satanic groups or emissaries or any of their associates, subjects or superiors, to harm or to take revenge on me, my family and my associates or cause harm or damage to anything we have.

In the Name of Jesus Christ and by the merits of His Precious Blood, I break and dissolve every curse, hex, seal, spell, sorcery, bond, snare, trap, device, lie, stumbling block, obstacle, deception, diversion or distraction, spiritual chain or spiritual influence, also every disease of body, soul, mind or spirit placed upon us or on this place, or on any of the persons, places things mentioned, by any agent, or brought on us by our own mistakes or sins. *(3x)*

I now place the cross of Jesus Christ between myself and all generations in my family tree. I say in the Name of Jesus Christ that there will be no direct communication between the generations. All communications will be filtered through the Precious Blood of the lord Jesus Christ. Mary the Immaculate, clothe me in the light, power and energy of your faith. Father, please assign the angels and saints to assist me. Thank you, Lord Jesus, for being my Wisdom, my Justice, my Sanctification, my Redemption.

I surrender to the ministry of Your Holy Spirit, and I receive Your truth concerning inter-generational healing.

Glory be to the Father, and to the Son, and to the Holy Spirit. As it was in the beginning, is now and ever shall be world without end.

WARFARE PRAYER

Heavenly Father, I bow in worship and praise before you. I cover myself with the blood of Jesus Christ. I claim the protection of the blood for my family, my finances, my home, my spirit, soul, and body. I surrender myself completely in every area of my life to you. I take a stand against all the workings of the devil that would try to hinder me and my family from best serving you. I address myself only in the True and Living God, who has all power and control over everything. In the name of Jesus Christ, I command you, satan, and all of your demon forces of darkness, to leave my presence. I plead the blood of Jesus Christ.

Furthermore, in my own life today, I destroy and tear down all the strongholds of the devil against my mind. I surrender my mind to you, blessed Holy Spirit. I affirm, Heavenly Father, that you have not given me the Spirit of fear but of power, and of love, and of a sound mind (II Timothy 1:7). Therefore, I resist the spirit of fear in the name of Jesus, the Son of the Living God. I refuse to doubt and refuse to worry because I have authority [power] over all the power of the enemy and nothing will hurt me (Luke 10:19). I claim complete and absolute victory over the forces of darkness in the Name of Jesus, and I bind the devil and command him to loose my peace, joy, prosperity and every member of my family for the glory of God and by faith I call it done.

I break and smash the strongholds satan formed against my emotions today. I give my body to you, Lord Jesus, realizing that I am the temple of the Holy Spirit (I Corinthians 3:16, I Corinthians 6:19-20). Again, I cover myself with the blood of the Lord Jesus Christ. I pray that the Holy Spirit would bring all the work of the crucifixion, all the work of the resurrection, all the work of the ascension of the Lord Jesus Christ into my life, today. I surrender my life and possessions to you. I refuse to fear, worry, or to be discouraged in the Name of Jesus. I will not hate, envy, or show any type of bitterness toward my brothers, sisters or my enemies. I will love them with the love God shed abroad in my heart by the Holy Spirit .

Open my eyes and show me the areas of my life that did not please you. Give me strength, grace, and wisdom to remove any sin or weight that would prevent our close fellowship. Work in me to cleanse me from all ground that would give the devil a foothold against me. I claim in every way the victory of the cross over all satanic forces in my life. I pray in the name of the Lord Jesus Christ with thanksgiving and I welcome all the ministry of the Holy Spirit.

AMEN

World Trade Center 9/11/01 **

PRAYERS AGAINST TERRORISM

"...be well versed in all that is good yet pure as to what is evil and God, the giver of peace, will crush Satan under your feet" (Rom 16:19-20).

Prayer of Protection against Terrorism

Loving Father, in humble trust we draw your attention to every act of violence and terrorism being planned for this city (state, country). Thank You for sending the Holy Spirit to expose and defeat weapons of destruction. We take authority in Jesus' Name over every planned act of violence and command it to wither and die. Father, forgive those who would seek to harm others and bring them into a healed relationship with our Lord Jesus. Thank You for protecting our city. Thank You for alerting many intercessors to pray a shield of protection around our city and around those individuals assigned to protect the people of our city. Holy Spirit, come. Release the peace of Christ into our city.

Thank You, Lord. Amen.

Prayer Against Terrorism

Prayer written by Rev. Murat Kuntel. He is a former Muslim, who is now minister of a Presbyterian Church in Canada.

Father, You are our protector. I pray that the victims of terrorism may find comfort in You, for You are our refuge. I pray that society may become one in goodness, and, in love, we may embrace all those who lost a loved one, especially a parent. I pray that our society may be transformed and reflect Your glory in the Trinity, as we become more caring for one another, as much as we are for our own interests. I pray that You would put a hedge around our homes, ourselves, our children and our loved ones, that wherever we go, no evil person or no evil whatsoever will be able to harm us.

I pray that You would hedge in the terrorists, who plan to harm innocent people, with mighty angels, that their hands be tied down, that their feet be stumbling, that their tongues be giving away their identity, that they may not be able to harm the innocent ones in any way, and that they be caught by the authorities.

I pray that there may be unity in the world against evil, that the world leaders may hear Your voice, choose good over evil, lead their nations in peace and for peace, and work together to bring peace to the world, tolerating differences of opinions, religions and races, but not tolerating evil.

I pray that the bondage of darkness in the hearts of these evil people be broken and instead their hearts be enlightened by Your truth and love, that they may not only give up their terrorism, but give their lives to You, our Father, through Your Son Jesus Christ, and be filled with Your Holy Spirit, so that they may live lives led by the Spirit, always seeking the good of others as well as their own, obedient to Your Word in all matters.

I pray that we, the Christians, may be revived; that we, as Your children in Christ, may willingly participate in the priestly ministry of Christ's intercession and reconciliation through the enabling Holy Spirit within us; and that we may intercede for the protection of loved ones, and for the correction and salvation of those who choose to be hostile against humanity.

I pray that You, by Your grace, may fill us with the fullness of Your Holy Spirit that we may enjoy the privileges of belonging to Your kingdom, and keep on interceding with perseverance and never give up loving all and doing good to all by the power of the Holy Spirit, Your glory, our Father in heaven, in the name of Your Son Jesus Christ our Lord.

Pentagon 9/11/01 ***

A Prayer for Attacks Against America

Gracious God, through your Son you have taught us that nothing in life or in death is able to separate us from your love. Look in mercy on all to whom great sorrow has come through the terrorism in America. Help those who are injured, support those who are dying. Strengthen the members of the emergency services, the military and all who bring relief and comfort. Console and protect those who have lost loved ones. Give your light in darkness to all who are near to despair, and assure them that you hold all souls in life; through Jesus Christ our risen Lord. Amen.

Prayers for the Peace in the World

Almighty God,
From whom all thoughts of truth and peace proceed: kindle, we pray, in the hearts of all people the true love of peace; and guide with your pure and peaceable wisdom those who take counsel for the nations of the earth; that in tranquillity your kingdom may go forward, till the earth is filled with the knowledge of your love; through Jesus Christ our Lord.
 Amen.

Eternal God, our only hope, our help in time of trouble: help the nations of the world to work out their differences. Do not let threats multiply, or power be used without compassion. May your word rule the words of world leaders, so that they may agree and settle claims peacefully. Restrain those who are impulsive, that desire for vengeance may not overwhelm our common welfare. Give peace in our time, O Lord; through Jesus Christ, the Prince of Peace and Saviour of us all.
Amen.

God of the nations,
whose kingdom rules over all: have mercy on our broken
and divided world. Shed abroad your peace in the hearts
of all people, and banish from them the spirit that makes
for war; that all races and peoples may learn to live as
members of one family, and in obedience to your laws;
through Jesus Christ our Lord.

Almighty God,
whose will is to restore all things in your beloved Son, the
king of all the world: govern the hearts and minds of
those in authority, and bring the families of the nations,
divided and torn apart by the ravages of sin, to be subject
to Christ's just and gentle rule; who is alive and reigns
with you and the Holy Spirit, one God, now and for ever.
Amen.

La Tour, Georges de c. 1635

OTHER WORLD PRAYERS

Psalm of Islam His Supplication Against Satan
(Supplication - 17)

O God,
we seek refuge in Thee
from the instigations of the accursed Satan,
his trickery, and his traps,
from trust in his false hopes, his promises,
his delusions, and his snares,

and lest he should make himself crave
to lead us away from Thy obedience
and to degrade us through our disobeying Thee,
and lest what he has shown us as beautiful be beautiful
for us
and what he has shown us as detestable weigh down
upon us.
O God,
drive him away from us through Thy worship,
throw him down through our perseverance in Thy love,
and place between him and us a covering
that he cannot tear away
and a solid barrier
that he cannot cut through!
O God,
bless Muhammad and his Household,
distract Satan from us with some of Thy
enemies, preserve us from him through Thy good
guarding, spare us his treachery,
turn his back toward us,
and cut off from us his trace!
O God,
bless Muhammad and his Household,
give us to enjoy guidance
the like of his misguidance,
increase us in piety against his seduction,
and make us walk in reverential fear
contrary to his path of ruin!
O God,
assign him no place of entrance into our hearts
and do not allow him to make his home in
that which is with us!
O God,

cause us to recognize the falsehood with which he
tempts us,
and once Thou hast caused us to recognize it,
protect us from it!
Make us see what will allow us to outwit him,
inspire us with all that we can make ready for him,
awaken us from the heedless slumber of relying upon
him, and help us well, through Thy giving success,
against him!
O God,
saturate our hearts with the rejection of his works
and be gentle to us by destroying his stratagems!
O God,
bless Muhammad and his Household,
turn his authority away from us,
cut off his hope from us,
and keep him from craving for us!
O God,
bless Muhammad and his Household,
and place our fathers, our mothers,
our children, our wives, our siblings, our relatives,
and the faithful among our neighbours,
male and female,
in a sanctuary impregnable to him,
a guarding fortress,
a defending cave!
Clothe them in shields protective against him and give
them arms that will cut him down!
O God,
include in that everyone who
witnesses to Thee as Lord,
devotes himself sincerely to Thy Unity,
shows enmity toward him

through the reality of servanthood,
and seeks help from Thee against him
through knowledge of the divine sciences!
O God,
undo what he ties,
unstitch what he sews up,
dislocate what he devises,
frustrate him when he makes up his mind,
and destroy what he establishes!
O God,
rout his troops, nullify his trickery,
make his cave collapse,
and rub his nose in the ground!
O God,
place us in the ranks of his enemies
and remove us from the number of his friends,
that we obey him not when he entices us
and answer him not when he calls to us!
We command everyone who obeys our command to be
his enemy
and we admonish everyone who follows our prohibition
not to follow him!
O God,
bless Muhammad,
the Seal of the prophets and lord of the emissaries, and
the folk of his house,
the good, the pure!
Give refuge to us, our families, our brothers,
and all the faithful, male and female,
from that from which we seek refuge,
and grant us sanctuary from that through
fear of which we seek sanctuary in Thee!
Hear our supplication to Thee,

bestow upon us that of which we have been heedless, and safeguard for us what we have forgotten! Through all this bring us into the ranks of the righteous and the degrees of the faithful!
Amen, Lord of the worlds!

Sacred Song of the Sikhs

May the passions of lust, anger, greed, pride and attachment depart from me.
O Lord, I come to seek Thy shelter.
Bless me with thy grace.

Tibetan Phowa

Through Your blessing, grace and guidance, from the power of the light that streams from You: may all my negative Karma,destructive emotions, obscurations and blockages be purified and removed. May I know myself forgiven for all the harm I may have thought and done. May I accomplish this profound practice of phowa, and die a good and peaceful death. And through the triumph of my death, may I be able to benefit all other beings, living and dead.

Hinduism - Brief Vedic Prayer

O! All powerful God. Thou art the protector of the whole physical creation, may Thou protect my body. Thou art the source of all life. Thou art the source of all strength, may thou make me strong. O, omnipotent Lord, I live to thee to fill up all my wants and to give me perfection, physical, mental and spiritual.

Rabbi Praying   Szymon Buchbinder c. 1908

Old Jewish prayer prayed by the ancient Rabbis.

"Lord deliver me from an evil accident, and diseases; and do not trouble me with evil dreams, and evil imaginations. let it be thy good pleasure, 0 Lord our God, and the God of our fathers, that thou wouldst deliver us from an evil man, and from an evil accident; from the evil imagination, i.e. the corruption of nature; from an evil companion; from an evil neighbor; and from Satan the destroyer; and from hard judgment; and from an hard adversary, whether he is the son of the covenant, or is not the son of the covenant."

Das Paradies des Buddha Amitabha 8th century

Buddhist Meditation for keeping evil away
(from the Sutta Nipata)

"The practice of Dhamma, the practice of continence, mastery of this is said to be best if a person has gone forth from home to the homeless life. But if he is garrulous and, like a brute, delights in hurting others, his life is evil and his impurity increases.

"A quarrelsome bhikkhu shrouded by delusion, does not comprehend the Dhamma taught by the Awakened One when it is revealed. Annoying those practiced in meditation, being led by ignorance, he is not aware that

63

his defiled path leads to Niraya-hell. Falling headlong, passing from womb to womb, from darkness to (greater) darkness, such a bhikkhu undergoes suffering hereafter for certain.

"As a cesspool filled over a number of years is difficult to clean, similarly, whoever is full of impurity is difficult to make pure. Whoever you know to be such, bhikkhus, bent on worldliness, having wrong desires, wrong thoughts, wrong behavior and resort, being completely united avoid him, sweep him out like dirt, remove him like rubbish. Winnow like chaff the non-recluses. Having ejected those of wrong desires, of wrong behavior and resort, be pure and mindful, dwelling with those who are pure. Being united and prudent you will make an end to suffering."

"Soul-Killing Witches that Deform the Body" – Shak, 1828

PRAYERS FOR PROTECTION FROM THE OCCULT

[9] When you enter the land the LORD your God is giving you, do not learn to imitate the detestable ways of the nations there. [10] Let no one be found among you who sacrifices his son or daughter in [1] the fire, who practices divination or sorcery, interprets omens, engages in witchcraft, or casts spells, or who is a medium or spiritist or who consults the dead." Deuteronomy 18:9-11

Below are warfare prayers to fight against voodoo, root workers, conjure men, root doctors, Haitian, African, Black Southern, and any other country Witchcraft.

PRAYER: In the Name of the Lord Jesus Christ, I take authority over all curses in my family line due to the practice of magic done by some ancestor in the past. I command prosperity to come forth on my business and family line, in the Name of Jesus Christ.

PRAYER: Father in the Name of the Lord Jesus, I command spirits of divination, familiar spirits and death spirits to come out of me in the name of the Lord Jesus Christ.

PRAYER: In the name of the Lord Jesus Christ, I bind evil spirits and cast them out of me in the Name of the Lord Jesus Christ. Also, I loose myself from the control and conjuration of the priest or priestess.

PRAYER: In the Name of the Lord Jesus Christ, I loose myself and my family members from any curses from my involvement in voodoo or black witchcraft. I command all related spirits to come out of me now, in the Name of Jesus Christ.

PRAYER: Father in the Name of the Lord Jesus Christ, I loose myself and my family line from curses that have come on me and my family due to me or my family members dealing with occult, voodoo, witchcraft and/or sorcery that has opened the door for demons to bind us. I cast them out in the Name of the Lord Jesus Christ.

PRAYER: In the Name of the Lord Jesus, I take authority over the strong man of the gris-gris (people who use curses) or grigri and command them to come out now. Also I command the objects used or sorcery used to loose its control and power over this person, family or congregation to leave now in Jesus' Name.

PRAYER: In the Name of the Lord Jesus Christ, I loose myself and my family from the ancestral or family line curse of the ruling Loa (voodoo spirit) (or other evil spirit) and I command it broken over us and I command all demons associated with it to come out now IN JESUS' NAME.

PRAYER: Father, in the Name of the Lord Jesus Christ, I command the spirits in the drums that conjure up demons to be broken and come out in the Name of Jesus Christ.

PRAYER: In the Name of the Lord Jesus, I command my soul to be loosed from the earthen vessel that holds it and put back in its proper place.

PRAYER: In the Name of the Lord Jesus, I take authority over the rulers of the bottomless pit and I command every African, Haitian or Black Voodoo curse to be broken in the Name of Jesus Christ, and command the cross roads to be closed to me and my family line forever. I command all demons associated with this curse to come out in Jesus' Name.

PRAYER: Father in the Name of the Lord Jesus Christ, I loose myself and my family line from curses coming against us from those working voodoo by burning candles, bowing down to idols, using psychic prayers and charms against me and my family line and cast these spirits out in the Name of the Lord Jesus Christ. I also loose myself and my family line from any curses and spirits that I or a family member have opened the door to attack us in the past and cast them out in the Name of the Lord Jesus Christ.

PRAYER: Father in the Name of the Lord Jesus Christ, I take authority over any curses that are being sent or that I or my family line have opened the door to by using scriptures to curse me or my family line. I cast these demons out in the Name of the Lord Jesus Christ.

PRAYER: Father in the Name of the Lord Jesus Christ, I take authority over spirits

of false prophecy, false gifts, and false inherited gifts of the spirit realm counterfeiting the Holy Ghost, false dreams and visions, I cast them out in the Name of the Lord Jesus Christ.

PRAYER: Father in the Name of the Lord Jesus Christ, I command the power in and over the fetish to be broken and I cast out every spirit that is operating in any object and break its power over me and my family line. Father in the Name of the Lord Jesus Christ, I cast out of me and my family line any demons that may have gained ground over our lives

St Francis Borgia Performing an Exorcism –
Francisco de Goya 1788

A Simple Exorcism for Priests or Laity

Prayer Against Satan and the Rebellious Angels by Order of His Holiness Pope Leo XIII

The following is a simple exorcism prayer that can be said by priests or laity. The term "**exorcism**" does NOT always denote a solemn exorcism involving a person possessed by the devil. In general, the term denotes prayers to "curb the power of the devil and prevent him from doing harm."

The Holy Father exhorts priests to say this prayer as often as possible, as a simple exorcism to curb the power of the devil and prevent him from doing harm. The faithful also may say it in their own name, for the same purpose, as any approved prayer. Its use is recommended whenever action of the devil is suspected, causing malice in men, violent temptations and even storms and various calamities. It could be used as a solemn exorcism (an official and public ceremony, in Latin), to expel the devil. A priest, in the name of the Church and only with a Bishop's permission, would then say it.

Prayer to St. Michael the Archangel

In the Name of the Father, and of the Son, and of the Holy Ghost. Amen.

Most glorious Prince of the Heavenly Armies, Saint Michael the Archangel, defend us in "our battle against principalities and powers, against the rulers of this world of darkness, against the spirits of wickedness in the high places" (Eph., 6,12). Come to the assistance of men whom God has created to His likeness and whom He has redeemed at a great price from the tyranny of the devil. Holy Church venerates thee as her guardian and protector; to thee, the Lord has entrusted the souls of the redeemed to be led into heaven. Pray therefore the God of Peace to crush Satan beneath our feet, that he may no longer retain men captive and do injury to the Church. Offer our prayers to the Most High, that without delay they may draw His mercy down upon us; take hold of "the dragon, the old serpent, which is the devil and Satan", bind him and cast him into the bottomless pit ... "that he may no longer seduce the nations" (Apoc. 20, 2-3).

Exorcism

In the Name of Jesus Christ, our God and Lord, strengthened by the intercession of the Immaculate Virgin Mary, Mother of God, of Blessed Michael the Archangel, of the Blessed Apostles Peter and Paul and all the Saints. (and powerful in the holy authority of our ministry)*, we confidently undertake to repulse the attacks and deceits of the devil.
*** *Lay people omit the parenthesis above.***

Psalm 67

God arises; His enemies are scattered and those who hate Him flee before Him. As smoke is driven away, so are they driven; as wax melts before the fire, so the wicked perish at the presence of God.

V. Behold the Cross of the Lord, flee bands of enemies.
R. The Lion of the tribe of Juda, the offspring of David, hath conquered.

V. May Thy mercy, Lord, descend upon us.
R. As great as our hope in Thee.

(The crosses below indicate a blessing to be given if a priest recites the Exorcism; if a lay person recites it, they indicate the Sign of the Cross to be made silently by that person.)

We drive you from us, whoever you may be, unclean spirits, all satanic powers, all infernal invaders, all wicked legions, assemblies and sects. In the Name and by the power of Our Lord Jesus Christ, + may you be snatched away and driven from the Church of God and from the souls made to the image and likeness of God and redeemed by the Precious Blood of the Divine Lamb. +

Most cunning serpent, you shall no more dare to deceive the human race, persecute the Church, torment God's elect and sift them as wheat. + The Most High God commands you, + He with whom, in your great insolence, you still claim to be equal. "God who wants all men to be saved and to come to the knowledge of the truth" (I Tim. 2,4). God the Father commands you. + God the Son commands you. + God the Holy Ghost commands you. + Christ, God's Word made flesh, commands you; + He who to save our race outdone through your envy, "humbled Himself, becoming obedient even unto death" (Phil.2,8); He who has built His Church on the firm rock and declared that the gates of hell shall not prevail against Her, because He will dwell with Her "all days even to the end of the world" (Matt. 28,20). The sacred Sign of the Cross commands you, + as does also the power of the mysteries of the Christian Faith. + The glorious Mother of God, the Virgin Mary, commands you; + she who by her humility and from the first moment of her Immaculate Conception crushed your proud head. The faith of the holy Apostles Peter and Paul, and of the other Apostles commands you. + The blood of the Martyrs and the pious intercession of all the Saints command you. +

Thus, cursed dragon, and you, diabolical legions, we adjure you by the living God, + by the true God, + by the holy God, + by the God "who so loved the world that He gave up His only Son, that every soul believing in Him might not perish but have life everlasting" (St.John 3, 16); stop deceiving human creatures and pouring out to them the poison of eternal damnation; stop harming the Church and hindering her liberty. Begone, Satan, inventor and master of all deceit, enemy of man's salvation. Give place to Christ in Whom you have found none of your works; give place to the One, Holy, Catholic and Apostolic Church acquired by Christ at the price of His Blood. Stoop beneath the all-powerful Hand of God; tremble and flee when we invoke the Holy and terrible Name of Jesus, this Name which causes hell to tremble, this Name to which the Virtues, Powers and Dominations of heaven are humbly submissive, this Name which the Cherubim and Seraphim praise unceasingly repeating: Holy, Holy, Holy is the Lord, the God of Hosts.

V. O Lord, hear my prayer.
R. And let my cry come unto Thee.
V. May the Lord be with thee.
R. And with thy spirit.

Let us pray.

God of heaven, God of earth, God of Angels, God of Archangels, God of Patriarchs, God of Prophets, God of Apostles, God of Martyrs, God of Confessors, God of Virgins, God who has power to give life after death and rest after work: because there is no other God than Thee and there can be no other, for Thou art the Creator of all things, visible and invisible, of Whose reign there shall be no end, we humbly prostrate ourselves before Thy glorious Majesty and we beseech Thee to deliver us by Thy power from all the tyranny of the infernal spirits, from their snares, their lies and their furious wickedness. Deign, O Lord, to grant us Thy powerful protection and to keep us safe and sound. We beseech Thee through Jesus Christ Our Lord. Amen.

V. From the snares of the devil,
R. Deliver us, O Lord.

V. That Thy Church may serve Thee in peace and liberty:
R. We beseech Thee to hear us.

V. That Thou may crush down all enemies of Thy Church:
R. We beseech Thee to hear us.

(Holy water is sprinkled in the place where we may be.)

Exorzismus an einer Frau - Mariazeller Wunderaltar 1519

Catholic Rite of Exorcism

The following is the Official Rite for expelling demons from people certified as being possessed by authorized Catholic priests.

RITE OF EXORCISM

The priest delegated by the Ordinary to perform this office should first go to confession or at least elicit an act of contrition, and, if convenient, offer the holy Sacrifice of the Mass, and implore God's help in other fervent prayers. He vests in surplice and purple stole. Having before him the person possessed (who should be bound if there is any danger), he traces the sign of the cross over him, over himself, and the bystanders, and then sprinkles all of them with holy water. After this he kneels and says the Litany of the Saints exclusive of the prayers, which follow it. All present are to make the responses.

LITANY OF THE SAINTS

The Litany of the Saints is used in ordination, Forty Hours', processions, and other occasions. Both the Roman Ritual and the Roman Pontifical direct that the first three invocations be repeated. The music for this litany is given in the music supplement. The invocations are sung (or recited) by the chanters or the priest; the responses by all.

P: Lord, have mercy.

All: Lord, have mercy.

P: Christ, have mercy.

All: Christ, have mercy.

P: Lord, have mercy.

All: Lord, have mercy.

P: Christ, hear us.

All: Christ, graciously hear us.

P: God, the Father in heaven.

All: Have mercy on us.

P: God, the Son, Redeemer of the world.

All: Have mercy on us.

P: God, the Holy Spirit.

All: Have mercy on us.

P: Holy Trinity, one God.

All: Have mercy on us.

Holy Mary, pray for us,*

*** After each invocation:*** "Pray for us."

Holy Mother of God,
Holy Virgin of virgins,
St. Michael,
St. Gabriel,
St. Raphael,
All holy angels and archangels,
All holy orders of blessed spirits,
St. John the Baptist,
St. Joseph,
All holy patriarchs and prophets,
St. Peter,
St. Paul,
St. Andrew,
St. James,
St. John,
St. Thomas,
St. James,
St. Philip,
St. Bartholomew,
St. Matthew,
St. Simon,
St. Thaddeus,
St. Matthias,
St. Barnabas,
St. Luke,
St. Mark,
All holy apostles and evangelists,
All holy disciples of the Lord,
All holy Innocents,
St. Stephen,
St. Lawrence,

St. Vincent,
SS. Fabian and Sebastian,
SS. John and Paul,
SS. Cosmas and Damian,
SS. Gervase and Protase,
All holy martyrs,
St. Sylvester,
St. Gregory,
St. Ambrose,
St. Augustine,
St. Jerome,
St. Martin,
St. Nicholas,
All holy bishops and confessors,
All holy doctors,
St. Anthony,
St. Benedict,
St. Bernard,
St. Dominic,
St. Francis,
All holy priests and levites,
All holy monks and hermits,
St. Mary Magdalen,
St. Agatha,
St. Lucy,
St. Agnes,
St. Cecilia,
St. Catherine,
St. Anastasia,
All holy virgins and widows,

P: All holy saints of God,

All: Intercede for us.

P: Be merciful,

All: Spare us, 0 Lord.

P: Be merciful,

All: Graciously hear us, 0 Lord.

From all evil, deliver us, 0 Lord.*

After each invocation: "Deliver us, 0 Lord."

From all sin,
From your wrath,
From sudden and unprovided death,
From the snares of the devil,
From anger, hatred, and all ill will,
From all lewdness,
From lightning and tempest,
From the scourge of earthquakes,
From plague, famine, and war,
From everlasting death,
By the mystery of your holy incarnation,
By your coming,
By your birth,
By your baptism and holy fasting,
By your cross and passion,

By your death and burial,
By your holy resurrection,
By your wondrous ascension,
By the coming of the Holy,
Spirit, the Advocate,
On the day of judgment,

P: We sinners,

All: We beg you to hear us.*

__After each invocation__: "We beg you to hear us."

That you spare us,
That you pardon us,
That you bring us to true penance,
That you govern and preserve your holy Church,
That you preserve our Holy Father and all ranks in the
Church in holy religion,

That you humble the enemies of holy Church,
That you give peace and true concord to all Christian
rulers.
That you give peace and unity to the whole Christian
world,
That you restore to the unity of the Church all who have
strayed from the truth, and lead all unbelievers to the light
of the Gospel,

That you confirm and preserve us in your holy service,
That you lift up our minds to heavenly desires,

81

That you grant everlasting blessings to all our benefactors,
That you deliver our souls and the souls of our brethren, relatives, and benefactors from everlasting damnation,

That you give and preserve the fruits of the earth,
That you grant eternal rest to all the faithful departed,
That you graciously hear us, Son of God,

At the end of the litany he (the priest) adds the following:

P: **Antiphon**: Do not keep in mind, 0 Lord, our offenses or those of our parents, nor take vengeance on our sins.

P: Our Father **the rest inaudibly until**

P: And lead us not into temptation.

All: But deliver us from evil.

Psalm 53

P: God, by your name save me, * and by your might defend my cause.

All: God, hear my prayer; * hearken to the words of my mouth.

P: For haughty men have risen up against me, and fierce men seek my life; *

they set not God before their eyes.

All: See, God is my helper; * the Lord sustains my life.

P: Turn back the evil upon my foes; * in your faithfulness destroy them.

All: Freely will I offer you sacrifice; * I will praise your name, Lord, for its goodness,

P: Because from all distress you have rescued me, * and my eyes look down upon my enemies.

All: Glory be to the Father.

P: As it was in the beginning.

After the psalm the priest continues:

P: Save your servant.

All: Who trusts in you, my God.

P: Let him (her) find in you, Lord, a fortified tower.

All: In the face of the enemy.

P: Let the enemy have no power over him (her).

All: And the son of iniquity be powerless to harm him (her).

P: Lord, send him (her) aid from your holy place.

All: And watch over him (her) from Sion.

P: Lord, heed my prayer.

All: And let my cry be heard by you.

P: The Lord be with you.

All: May He also be with you.

Let us pray Pray

God, whose nature is ever merciful and forgiving, accept our prayer that this servant of yours, bound by the fetters of sin, may be pardoned by your loving kindness.

Holy Lord, almighty Father, everlasting God and Father of our Lord Jesus Christ, who once and for all consigned that fallen and apostate tyrant to the flames of hell, who sent your only-begotten Son into the world to crush that roaring lion; hasten to our call for help and snatch from ruination and from the clutches of the noonday devil this human being made in your image and likeness.

Strike terror, Lord, into the beast now laying waste your vineyard. Fill your servants with courage to fight manfully against that reprobate dragon, lest he despise those who put their trust in you, and say with Pharaoh of old: "I know not God, nor will I set Israel free." Let your mighty hand cast him out of your servant, **N.**, ✝ so he may no longer hold captive this person whom it pleased you to make in your image, and to redeem through your Son; who lives and reigns with you, in the unity of the Holy Spirit, God, forever and ever.

All: Amen.

Then he commands the demon as follows:

I command you, unclean spirit, whoever you are, along with all your minions now attacking this servant of God, by the mysteries of the incarnation, passion, resurrection, and ascension of our Lord Jesus Christ, by the descent of the Holy Spirit, by the coming of our Lord for judgment, that you tell me by some sign your name, and the day and hour of your departure. I command you, moreover, to obey me to the letter, I who am a minister of God despite my unworthiness; nor shall you be emboldened to harm in any way this creature of God, or the bystanders, or any of their possessions.

The priest lays his hand on the head of the sick person, saying:

They shall lay their hands upon the sick and all will be well with them. May Jesus, Son of Mary, Lord and Savior of the world, through the merits and intercession of His holy apostles Peter and Paul and all His saints, show you favor and mercy.

All: Amen.

Next he reads over the possessed person these selections from the Gospel, or at least one of them.

P: The Lord be with you.

All: May He also be with you.

P: The beginning of the holy Gospel according to St. John.

All: Glory be to you, 0 Lord.

A Lesson from the holy Gospel according to St. John

John 1.1-14

As he says these opening words he signs himself and the possessed on the brow, lips, and breast.

When time began, the Word was there, and the Word was face to face with God, and the Word was God. This Word, when time began, was face to face with God. All things came into being through Him, and without Him there came to be not one thing that has come to be. In Him was life, and the life was the light of men. The light shines in the darkness, and the darkness did not lay hold of it. There came upon the scene a man, a messenger from God, whose name was John. This man came to give testimony to testify in behalf of the light that all might believe through him. He was not himself the light; he only was to testify in behalf of the light. Meanwhile the true light, which illumines every man, was making its entrance into the world. He was in the world, and the world came to be through Him, and the world did not acknowledge Him. He came into His home, and His own people did not welcome Him. But to as many as welcomed Him He gave the power to become children of God those who believe in His name; who were born not of blood, or of carnal desire, or of man's will; no, they were born of God. (Genuflect here.) And the Word became man and lived among us; and we have looked upon His glory such a glory as befits the Father's only-begotten Son full of grace and truth!

All: Thanks be to God.

Lastly he blesses the sick person, saying:

May the blessing of almighty God, Father, Son, ✝ and Holy Spirit, come upon you and remain with you forever.

All: Amen.

Then he sprinkles the person with holy water.

A Lesson from the holy Gospel according to St. Mark

Mark 16.15-18

At that time Jesus said to His disciples: "Go into the whole world and preach the Gospel to all creation. He that believes and is baptized will be saved; he that does not believe will be condemned. And in the way of proofs of their claims, the following will accompany those who believe: in my name they will drive out demons; they will speak in new tongues; they will take up serpents in their hands, and if they drink something deadly, it will not hurt them; they will lay their hands on the sick, and these will recover."

A Lesson from the holy Gospel according to St. Luke

Luke 10.17-20

At that time the seventy-two returned in high spirits. "Master," they said, "even the demons are subject to us because we use your name!" "Yes," He said to them, "I was watching Satan fall like lightning that flashes from heaven. But mind: it is I that have given you the power to tread upon serpents and scorpions, and break the dominion of the enemy everywhere; nothing at all can injure you. Just the same, do not rejoice in the fact that the spirits are subject to you, but rejoice in the fact that your names are engraved in heaven."

A Lesson from the holy Gospel according to St. Luke

Luke 11.14-22

At that time Jesus was driving out a demon, and this particular demon was dumb. The demon was driven out, the dumb man spoke, and the crowds were enraptured. But some among the people remarked: "He is a tool of Beelzebul, and that is how he drives out demons!" Another group, intending to test Him, demanded of Him a proof of His claims, to be shown in the sky. He knew their inmost thoughts. "Any kingdom torn by civil strife," He said to them, "is laid in ruins; and house tumbles upon house. So, too, if Satan is in revolt against himself, how can his kingdom last, since you say that I drive out demons as a tool of Beelzebul. And furthermore: if I drive out demons as a tool of Beelzebul, whose tools are your pupils when they do the driving out? Therefore, judged by them, you must stand condemned. But, if, on the contrary, I drive out demons by the finger of God, then, evidently the kingdom of God has by this time made its way to you. As long as a mighty lord in full armor guards his premises, he is in peaceful possession of his property; but should one mightier than he attack and overcome him, he will strip him of his armor, on which he had relied, and distribute the spoils taken from him."

P: Lord, heed my prayer.

All: And let my cry be heard by you.

P: The Lord be with you.

All: May He also be with you.

Let us pray.

Almighty Lord, Word of God the Father, Jesus Christ, God and Lord of all creation; who gave to your holy apostles the power to tramp underfoot serpents and scorpions; who along with the other mandates to work miracles was pleased to grant them the authority to say: "Depart, you devils!" and by whose might Satan was made to fall from heaven like lightning; I humbly call on your holy name in fear and trembling, asking that you grant me, your unworthy servant, pardon for all my sins, steadfast faith, and the power — supported by your mighty arm — to confront with confidence and resolution this cruel demon. I ask this through you, Jesus Christ, our Lord and God, who are coming to judge both the living and the dead and the world by fire.

All: Amen.

Next he makes the sign of the cross over himself and the one possessed, places the end of the stole on the latter's neck, and, putting his right hand on the latter's head, he says the following in accents filled with confidence and faith:

P: See the cross of the Lord; begone, you hostile powers!

All: The stem of David, the lion of Juda's tribe has conquered.

P: Lord, heed my prayer.

All: And let my cry be heard by you.

P: The Lord be with you.

All: May He also be with you.

Let us pray.

God and Father of our Lord Jesus Christ, I appeal to your holy name, humbly begging your kindness, that you graciously grant me help against this and every unclean spirit now tormenting this creature of yours; through Christ our Lord.

All: Amen.

Exorcism

I cast you out, unclean spirit, along with every Satanic power of the enemy, every spectre from hell, and all your fell companions; in the name of our Lord Jesus ✠ Christ. Begone and stay far from this creature of God. ✠ For it is He who commands you, He who flung you headlong from the heights of heaven into the depths of hell. It is He who commands you, He who once stilled the sea and the wind and the storm. Hearken, therefore, and tremble in fear, Satan, you enemy of the faith, you foe of the human race, you begetter of death, you robber of life, you corrupter of justice, you root of all evil and vice; seducer of men, betrayer of the nations, instigator of envy, font of avarice, fomentor of discord, author of pain and sorrow. Why, then, do you stand and resist, knowing as you must that Christ the Lord brings your plans to nothing? Fear Him, who in Isaac was offered in sacrifice, in Joseph sold into bondage, slain as the paschal lamb, crucified as man, yet triumphed over the powers of hell. *(The three signs of the cross which follow are traced on the brow of the possessed person).* Begone, then, in the name of the Father, ✠ and of the Son, ✠ and of the Holy ✠ Spirit. Give place to the Holy Spirit by this sign of the holy ✠ cross of our Lord Jesus Christ, who lives and reigns with the Father and the Holy Spirit, God, forever and ever.

All: Amen.

P: Lord, heed my prayer.

All: And let my cry be heard by you.

P: The Lord be with you.

All: May He also be with you.

Let us pray.

God, Creator and defender of the human race, who made man in your own image, look down in pity on this your servant, **N.**, now in the toils of the unclean spirit, now caught up in the fearsome threats of man's ancient enemy, sworn foe of our race, who befuddles and stupefies the human mind, throws it into terror, overwhelms it with fear and panic. Repel, 0 Lord, the devil's power, break asunder his snares and traps, put the unholy tempter to flight. By the sign ✠ **(on the brow)** of your name, let your servant be protected in mind and body. *(The three crosses which follow are traced on the breast of the possessed person).* Keep watch over the inmost recesses of his (her) ✠ heart; rule over his (her) ✠ emotions; strengthen his (her) ✠ will. Let vanish from his (her) soul the temptings of the mighty adversary. Graciously grant, 0 Lord, as we call on your holy name, that the evil spirit, who hitherto terrorized over us, may himself retreat in terror and defeat, so that this servant of yours may sincerely and steadfastly render you the service which is your due; through Christ our Lord.

All: Amen.

Exorcism

I adjure you, ancient serpent, by the judge of the living and the dead, by your Creator, by the Creator of the whole universe, by Him who has the power to consign you to hell, to depart forthwith in fear, along with your savage minions, from this servant of God, **N.**, who seeks refuge in the fold of the Church. I adjure you again, ✠ *(on the brow)* not by my weakness but by the might of the Holy Spirit, to depart from this servant of God, **N.** , whom almighty God has made in His image. Yield, therefore, yield not to my own person but to the minister of Christ. For it is the power of Christ that compels you, who brought you low by His cross. Tremble before that mighty arm that broke asunder the dark prison walls and led souls forth to light. May the trembling that afflicts this human frame, ✠ *(on the breast)* the fear that afflicts this image ✠ *(on the brow*) of God, descend on you. Make no resistance nor delay in departing from this man, for it has pleased Christ to dwell in man. Do not think of despising my command because you know me to be a great sinner. It is God ✠ Himself who commands you; the majestic Christ ✠ who commands you. God the Father ✠ commands you; God the Son ✠ commands you; God the Holy ✠ Spirit commands you. The mystery of the cross commands ✠ you. The faith of the holy apostles Peter and Paul and of all the saints commands ✠ you. The blood of the martyrs commands ✠ you. The continence of the confessors commands ✠ you. The devout prayers of all holy men and women command ✠ you. The saving mysteries of our Christian faith command ✠ you.

Depart, then, transgressor. Depart, seducer, full of lies and cunning, foe of virtue, persecutor of the innocent. Give place, abominable creature, give way, you monster, give way to Christ, in whom you found none of your works. For He has already stripped you of your powers and laid waste your kingdom, bound you prisoner and plundered your weapons. He has cast you forth into the outer darkness, where everlasting ruin awaits you and your abettors. To what purpose do you insolently resist? To what purpose do you brazenly refuse? For you are guilty before almighty God, whose laws you have transgressed. You are guilty before His Son, our Lord Jesus Christ, whom you presumed to tempt, whom you dared to nail to the cross. You are guilty before the whole human race, to whom you prof erred by your enticements the poisoned cup of death.

Therefore, I adjure you, profligate dragon, in the name of the spotless ✠ Lamb, who has trodden down the asp and the basilisk, and overcome the lion and the dragon, to depart from this man (woman) ✠ *(on the brow)*, to depart from the Church of God ✠ (*signing the bystanders*). Tremble and flee, as we call on the name of the Lord, before whom the denizens of hell cower, to whom the heavenly Virtues and Powers and Dominations are subject, whom the Cherubim and Seraphim praise with unending cries as they sing: Holy, holy, holy, Lord God of Sabaoth. The Word made flesh ✠ commands you; the Virgin's Son ✠ commands you; Jesus ✠ of Nazareth commands you, who once, when you despised His disciples, forced you to flee in shameful defeat from a man; and when He had cast you out you did not even dare, except by His leave, to enter into a herd of swine. And now as I adjure you in His ✠ name, begone from this man (woman) who is His creature. It is futile to resist His ✠ will. It is hard for you to kick against the ✠ goad. The longer you delay, the heavier your punishment shall be; for it is not men you are condemning, but rather Him who rules the living and the dead, who is coming to judge both the living and the dead and the world by fire.

All: Amen.

P: Lord, heed my prayer.

All: And let my cry be heard by you.

P: The Lord be with you.

All: May He also be with you.

Let us pray.

God of heaven and earth, God of the angels and archangels, God of the prophets and apostles, God of the martyrs and virgins, God who have power to bestow life after death and rest after toil; for there is no other God than you, nor can there be another true God beside you, the Creator of heaven and earth, who are truly a King, whose kingdom is without end; I humbly entreat your glorious majesty to deliver this servant of yours from the unclean spirits; through Christ Our Lord

All: Amen.

Exorcism

Therefore, I adjure you every unclean spirit, every spectre from hell, every satanic power, in the name of Jesus ✠ Christ of Nazareth, who was led into the desert after His baptism by John to vanquish you in your citadel, to cease your assaults against the creature whom He has, formed from the slime of the earth for His own honor and glory; to quail before wretched man, seeing in him the image of almighty God, rather than his state of human frailty. Yield then to God, ✠ who by His servant, Moses, cast you and your malice, in the person of Pharaoh and his army, into the depths of the sea. Yield to God, ✠ who, by the singing of holy canticles on the part of David, His faithful servant, banished you from the heart of King Saul. Yield to God, ✠ who condemned you in the person of Judas Iscariot, the traitor. For He now flails you with His divine scourges, ✠ He in whose sight you and your legions once cried out: "What have we to do with you, Jesus, Son of the Most High God? Have you come to torture us before the time?" Now He is driving you back into the everlasting fire, He who at the end of time will say to the wicked: "Depart from me, you accursed, into the everlasting fire which has been prepared for the devil and his angels." For you, 0 evil one, and for your followers there will be worms that never die. An unquenchable fire stands ready for you and for your minions, you prince of accursed murderers, father of lechery, instigator of sacrileges, model of vileness, promoter of heresies, inventor of every obscenity.

Depart, then, ✠ impious one, depart, ✠ accursed one, depart with all your deceits, for God has willed that man should be His temple. Why do you still linger here? Give honor to God the Father ✠ almighty, before whom every knee must bow. Give place to the Lord Jesus ✠ Christ, who shed His most precious blood for man. Give place to the Holy ✠ Spirit, who by His blessed apostle Peter openly struck you down in the person of Simon Magus; who cursed your lies in Annas and Saphira; who smote you in King Herod because he had not given honor to God; who by His apostle Paul afflicted you with the night of blindness in the magician Elyma, and by the mouth of the same apostle bade you to go out of Pythonissa, the soothsayer. Begone, ✠ now! Begone, ✠ seducer! Your place is in solitude; your abode is in the nest of serpents; get down and crawl with them. This matter brooks no delay; for see, the Lord, the ruler comes quickly, kindling fire before Him, and it will run on ahead of Him and encompass His enemies in flames. You might delude man, but God you cannot mock. It is He who casts you out, from whose sight nothing is hidden. It is He who repels you, to whose might all things are subject. It is He who expels you, He who has prepared everlasting hellfire for you and your angels, from whose mouth shall come a sharp sword, who is coming to judge both the living and the dead and the world by fire.

All: Amen.

All the above may be repeated as long as necessary, until the one possessed has been fully freed. It will also help to say devoutly and often over the afflicted person the Our Father, Hail Mary, and the Creed, as well as any of the prayers given below: The Canticle of our Lady, with the doxology; the Canticle of Zachary, with the doxology.

P: Antiphon: Magi from the East came to Bethlehem to adore the Lord; and opening their treasure chests they presented Him with precious gifts: Gold for the great King, incense for the true God, and myrrh in symbol of His burial. Alleluia.

Canticle of Our Lady (The Magnificat)
Luke 1:46 55

P: "My soul * extols the Lord;
All: And my spirit leaps for joy in God my Savior.
P: How graciously He looked upon His lowly maid! * Oh, see, from this hour
onward age after age will call me blessed!

All: How sublime is what He has done for me, * the Mighty One, whose name is `Holy'!

P: From age to age He visits those * who worship Him in reverence.

All: His arm achieves the mastery: * He routs the haughty and proud of heart.

P: He puts down princes from their thrones, * and exalts the lowly;

All: He fills the hungry with blessings, * and sends away the rich with empty hands.

P: He has taken by the hand His servant Israel, * and mercifully kept His faith,
All: As He had promised our fathers * with Abraham and his posterity forever
and evermore."

P: Glory be to the Father.
All: As it was in the beginning.

Antiphon: Magi from the East came to Bethlehem to adore the Lord; and opening their treasure chests they presented Him with precious gifts: Gold for the great King, incense for the true God, and myrrh in symbol of His burial. Alleluia.

Meanwhile the home is sprinkled with holy water and incensed. Then the priest says:

P: Our Father *the rest inaudibly until:*
P: And lead us not into temptation.

All: But deliver us from evil.

P: Many shall come from Saba.

All: Bearing gold and incense.

P: Lord, heed my prayer.

All: And let my cry be heard by you.

P: The Lord be with you.

All: May he also be with you.

Let us pray.

God, who on this day revealed your only-begotten Son to all nations by the guidance of a star, grant that we who now know you by faith may finally behold you in your heavenly majesty; through Christ our Lord.

All: Amen.

Responsory: Be enlightened and shine forth, 0 Jerusalem, for your light is come; and upon you is risen the glory of the Lord Jesus Christ born of the Virgin Mary.
P: Nations shall walk in your light, and kings in the splendor of your birth.
All: And the glory of the Lord is risen upon you.
Let us pray.

Lord God almighty, bless ✝ this home, and under its shelter let there be health, chastity, self-conquest, humility, goodness, mildness, obedience to your commandments, and thanksgiving to God the Father, Son, and Holy Spirit. May your blessing remain always in this home and on those who live here; through Christ our Lord.

All: Amen.

Antiphon for Canticle of Zachary:
Today the Church is espoused to her heavenly bridegroom, for Christ washes her sins in the Jordan; the Magi hasten with gifts to the regal nuptials; and the guests are gladdened with water made wine, alleluia.

Canticle of Zachary
Luke 1:68 79

P: "Blessed be the Lord, the God of Israel! * He has visited His people and
brought about its redemption.

All: He has raised for us a stronghold of salvation * in the house of David His servant,

P: And redeemed the promise He had made * through the mouth of His holy prophets of old
All: To grant salvation from our foes * and from the hand of all that hate us;

P: To deal in mercy with our fathers * and be mindful of His holy covenant,

All: Of the oath he had sworn to our father Abraham, * that He would enable us

P: Rescued from the clutches of our foes * to worship Him without fear,

All: In holiness and observance of the Law, * in His presence, all our days.

P: And you, my little one, will be hailed `Prophet of the Most High'; * for the
Lord's precursor you will be to prepare His ways;

All: You are to impart to His people knowledge of salvation * through forgiveness of their sins.
P: Thanks be to the merciful heart of our God! * a dawning Light from on high
will visit us

All: To shine upon those who sit in darkness and in the shadowland of death, * and guide our feet into the path of peace."

P: Glory be to the Father.
All: As it was in the beginning.

Antiphon:
Today the Church is espoused to her heavenly bridegroom, for Christ washes her sins in the Jordan; the Magi hasten with gifts to the regal nuptials; and the guests are gladdened with water made wine, alleluia.

Then the celebrant sings:

P: The Lord be with you.

All: May He also be with you.

P: Let us pray.

God, who on this day revealed your only-begotten Son to all nations by the guidance of a star, grant that we who now know you by faith may finally behold you in your heavenly majesty; through Christ our Lord.

All: Amen.

Athanasian Creed

P: Whoever wills to be saved * must before all else hold fast to the Catholic faith.

All: Unless one keeps this faith whole and untarnished, * without doubt he will perish forever.

P: Now this is the Catholic faith: * that we worship one God in Trinity, and Trinity in unity;

All: Neither confusing the Persons one with the other, * nor making a distinction in their nature.

P: For the Father is a distinct Person; and so is the Son; * and so is the Holy Spirit.

All: Yet the Father, Son, and Holy Spirit possess one Godhead, * co-equal glory, co-eternal majesty.

P: As the Father is, so is the Son, * so also is the Holy Spirit.

All: The Father is uncreated, the Son is uncreated, * the Holy Spirit is uncreated.

P: The Father is infinite, the Son is infinite, * the Holy Spirit is infinite.

All: The Father is eternal, the Son is eternal, * the Holy Spirit is eternal.

P: Yet they are not three eternals, * but one eternal God.

All: Even as they are not three uncreated, or three infinites, * but one uncreated and one infinite God.

P: So likewise the Father is almighty, the Son is almighty, * the Holy Spirit is almighty.

All: Yet they are not three almighties, * but they are the one Almighty.

P: Thus the Father is God, the Son is God, * the Holy Spirit is God.

All: Yet they are not three gods, * but one God.

P: Thus the Father is Lord, the Son is Lord, * the Holy Spirit is Lord.
All: Yet there are not three lords, * but one Lord.

P: For just as Christian truth compels us to profess that each Person is Individually God and Lord, * so does the Catholic religion forbid us to hold that there are three gods or lords.

All: The Father was not made by any power; * He was neither created nor begotten.

P: The Son is from the Father alone, * neither created nor made, but begotten.
All: The Holy Spirit is from the Father and the Son, * neither made nor created nor begotten, but He proceeds.

P: So there is one Father, not three; one Son, not three; * one Holy Spirit, not three.

All: And in this Trinity one Person is not earlier or later, nor is one greater or less; * but all three Persons are co-eternal and co-equal.

P: In every way, then, as already affirmed, * unity in Trinity and Trinity in unity is to be worshiped.

All: Whoever, then, wills to be saved * must assent to this doctrine of the Blessed Trinity.

P: But it is necessary for everlasting salvation * that one also firmly believe in The incarnation of our Lord Jesus Christ.

All: True faith, then, requires us to believe and profess * that our Lord Jesus Christ, the Son of God, is both God and man.

P: He is God, begotten of the substance of the Father from eternity; * He is man, born in time of the substance of His Mother.

All: He is perfect God, and perfect man * subsisting in a rational soul and a human body.

P: He is equal to the Father in His divine nature, * but less than the Father in His human nature as such.

All: And though He is God and man, * yet He is the one Christ, not two;

P: One, however, not by any change of divinity into flesh, * but by the act of God assuming a human nature.

All: He is one only, not by a mixture of substance, * but by the oneness of His Person.

P: For, somewhat as the rational soul and the body compose one man, * so Christ is one Person who is both God and man;

All: Who suffered for our salvation, who descended into hell, * who rose again the third day from the dead;
P: Who ascended into heaven, and sits at the right hand of God the Father almighty, * from there He shall come to judge both the living and the dead.

All: At His coming all men shall rise again in their bodies, * and shall give an account of their works.

P: And those who have done good shall enter into everlasting life, * but those who have done evil into everlasting fire.

All: All this is Catholic faith, * and unless one believes it truly and firmly one cannot be saved.

P: Glory be to the Father

All: As it was in the beginning.

Here follow a large number of psalms which may be used at the exorcist's discretion but are not a necessary part of the rite. Some of them occur in other parts of the Ritual and are so indicated; the others may be taken from the Psalter. Psalm 90 (see p. 227); psalm 67; psalm 69; psalm 53 (see p. 559); psalm 117 (see p. 248); psalm 34; psalm 30; psalm 21; psalm 3; psalm 10; psalm 12.

Prayer Following Deliverance

P: Almighty God, we beg you to keep the evil spirit from further molesting this servant of yours, and to keep him far away, never to return. At your command, 0 Lord, may the goodness and peace of our Lord Jesus Christ, our Redeemer, take possession of this man (woman). May we no longer fear any evil since the Lord is with us; who lives and reigns with you, in the unity of the Holy Spirit, God,
forever and ever.

All: Amen.

EXORCISM OF SATAN AND THE FALLEN ANGELS

*Whereas the **preceding rite** of exorcism is designated for a particular person, the present one is for general use --- to combat the power of the evil spirits over **a community or locality**. The following exorcism can be used by bishops, as well as by priests who have this authorization from their Ordinary.*

P: In the name of the Father, and of the Son, and of the Holy Spirit. Amen.

Prayer to St. Michael the Archangel

St. Michael the Archangel, illustrious leader of the heavenly army, defend us in the battle against principalities and powers, against the rulers of the world of darkness and the spirit of wickedness in high places. Come to the rescue of mankind, whom God has made in His own image and likeness, And purchased from Satan's tyranny at so great a price. Holy Church venerates you as her patron and guardian. The Lord has entrusted to you the task of leading the souls of the redeemed to heavenly blessedness. Entreat the Lord of peace to cast Satan down under our feet, so as to keep him from further holding man captive and doing harm to the Church. Carry our prayers up to God's throne, that the mercy of the Lord may quickly come and lay hold of the beast, the serpent of old, Satan and his demons, casting him in chains into the abyss, so that he can no longer seduce the nations.

Exorcism

P: In the name of Jesus Christ, our Lord and God, by the intercession of Mary, spotless Virgin and Mother of God, of St. Michael the Archangel, of the blessed apostles Peter and Paul, and of all the saints, and by the authority residing in our holy ministry, we steadfastly proceed to combat the onslaught of the wily enemy.

Psalm 67(8)

P: God arises; His enemies are scattered, * and those who hate Him flee before Him.

All: As smoke is driven away, so are they driven; * as wax melts before the fire, so the wicked perish before God.

P: See the cross of the Lord; begone, you hostile powers!

All: The stem of David, the lion of Juda's tribe has conquered.

P: May your mercy, Lord, remain with us always.

All: For we put our whole trust in you.

We cast you out, every unclean spirit, every satanic power, every onslaught of the infernal adversary, every legion, every diabolical group and sect, in the name and by the power of our Lord Jesus ✠ Christ. We command you, begone and fly far from the Church of God, from the souls made by God in His image and redeemed by the precious blood of the divine Lamb. ✠ No longer dare, cunning serpent, to deceive the human race, to persecute God's Church, to strike God's elect and to sift them as wheat. ✠ For the Most High God commands you, ✠ He to whom you once proudly presumed yourself equal; He who wills all men to be saved and come to the knowledge of truth. God the Father ✠ commands you. God the Son ✠ commands you. God the Holy ✠ Spirit commands you. Christ, the eternal Word of God made flesh, commands ✠ you, who humbled Himself, becoming obedient even unto death, to save our race from the perdition wrought by your envy; who founded His Church upon a firm rock, declaring that the gates of hell should never prevail against her, and that He would remain with her all days, even to the end of the world. The sacred mystery of the cross ✠ commands you, along with the power of all mysteries of Christian faith. ✠ The exalted Virgin Mary, Mother of God, ✠ commands you, who in her lowliness crushed your proud head from the first moment of her Immaculate Conception. The faith of the holy apostles Peter and Paul and the other apostles ✠ commands you. The blood of martyrs and the devout prayers of all holy men and women command ✠ you. Therefore, accursed dragon and every diabolical legion, we adjure you by the living ✠ God, by the true ✠ God, by the holy ✠ God, by God, who so loved the world that He gave His only-begotten Son, that whoever Believes in

Him might not perish but have everlasting life; to cease deluding human creatures and filling them with the poison of everlasting damnation; to desist from harming the Church and hampering her freedom. Begone, Satan, father and master of lies, enemy of man's welfare. Give place to Christ, in whom you found none of your works. Give way to the one, holy, catholic, and apostolic Church, which Christ Himself purchased with His blood. Bow down before God's mighty hand, tremble and flee as we call on the holy and awesome name of Jesus, before ehom the denizens of hell cower, to whom the heavenly Virtues and Powers and Dominations are subject, whom the Cherubim and Seraphim praise with unending cries as they sing: Holy, holy, holy, Lord God of Sabaoth.

P: Lord, heed my prayer.

All: And let my cry be heard by you.

P: The Lord be with you.

All: May He also be with you.

Let us pray.

God of heaven and earth, God of the angels and archangels, God of the patriarchs and prophets, God of the apostles and martyrs, God of the confessors and virgins, God who have power to bestow life after death and rest after toil; for there is no other God than you, nor can there be another true God beside you, the Creator of all things visible and invisible, whose kingdom is without end; we humbly entreat your glorious majesty to deliver us by your might from every influence of the accursed spirits, from their every evil snare and deception, and to keep us from all harm; through

Christ our Lord.

All: Amen.

P: From the snares of the devil.

All: Lord, deliver us.

P: That you help your Church to serve you in security and freedom.

All: We beg you to hear us.

P: That you humble the enemies of holy Church.

All: We beg you to hear us.

The surroundings are sprinkled with holy water.

St.Catherine of Sienna Exorcising a Possessed Woman
Benvenuto di Giovanni c. 1510

Catholic Rite of Exorcism - Latin Version

EXORCISMUS IN SATANAM ET ANGELOS
APOSTATICOS
Jussu Leonis Pp. XIII editus
Acta Sanctae Sedis vol. XXIII

Sequens exorcismus recitari potest ab Episcopis, nec non a Sacerdotibus, qui ab Ordinariis suis ad id auctoritatem habeant.

In nomine Patris, et Filii, **+** et Spiritus Sancti. Amen.

Ps. LXVII.

Exsurgat Deus et dissipentur inimici ejus: et fugiant qui oderunt eum a facie ejus.
Sicut deficit fumus, deficiant: sicut fluit cera a facie ignis, sic pereant peccatores a facie Dei.

Ps. XXXIV.

Judica, Domine, nocentes me: expugna impugnantes me.
Confundantur et revereantur quaerentes animam meam.
Avertantur retrorsum et confundantur cogitantes mihi mala.
Fiat tamquam pulvis ante faciem venti: et angelus Domini coarctans eos.
Fiat viae illorum tenebrae, et lubricum: et angelus Domini persequens eos.
Quoniam gratis absconderunt mihi interitum laquei sui: supervacue exprobraverunt animam meam.
Veniat illi laqueus quem ignorat; et captio quam anscondit, apprehendat eum: et in laqueum cadat in ipsum.
Anima autem meam exsultabit in Domino: et delectabitur super salutari suo.

Ad Sanctum Michaëlem Archangelum.
Precatio.

Princeps gloriosissime cælestis militiæ, sancte Michaël Archangele, defende nos in prælio et colluctatione, quæ nobis adversus principes et potestates, adversus mundi rectores tenebrarum harum, contra spiritualia nequitiæ, in cælestibusus. Veni in auxilium hominum, quos Deus creavit inexterminabiles, et ad imaginem similitudinis suæ fecit, et a tyrannide diaboli emit pretio magno. Præliare hodie cum beatorum Angelorum exercitu prælia Domini, sicut pugnasti contra ducem superbiæ luciferum, et angelos ejus apostaticos: et non valuerunt, neque locus inventus est eorum amplius in coelo. Sed projectus est draco ille magnus, serpens antiquus, qui vocatur diabolus et satanas, qui seducit universum orbem; et projectus est in terram, et angeli ejus cum illo missi sunt.

En antiquus inimicus et homicida vehementer erectus est. Transfiguratus in angelum lucis, cum tota malignorum spirituum caterva late circuit et invadit terram, ut in ea deleat nomen Dei et Christi ejus, animasque ad æternæ gloriæ coronam destinatas furetur, mactet ac perdat in sempiternum interitum. Virus nequitiæ suæ, tamquam flumen immundissimum, draco maleficus transfundit in homines depravatos mente et corruptos corde; spiritum mendacii, impietatis et blasphemiæ; halitumque mortiferum luxuriæ, vitiorum omnium et iniquitatum.

[Ecclesiam, Agni immaculati sponsam, faverrrimi hostes repleverunt amaritudinibus, inebriarunt absinthio; ad omnia desiderabilia ejus impias miserunt manus. Ubi sedes beatissimi Petri et Cathedra veritatis ad lucem gentium constituta est, ibi thronum posuerunt abominationis et impietatis suæ; ut percusso Pastore, et gregem disperdere valeant.]

Adesto itaque, Dux invictissime, populo Dei contra irrumpentes spirituales nequitias, et fac victoriam. Te custodem et patronum sancta veneratur Ecclesia; te gloriatur defensore adversus terrestrium et infernorum nefarias potestates; tibi tradidit Dominus animas redemptorum in superna felicitate locandas. Deprecare Deum pacis, ut conterat satanam sub pedibus nostris, ne ultra valeat captivos tenere homines, et Ecclesiæ nocere. Offer nostras preces in conspectu Altissimi, ut cito anticipent nos misericordiæ Domini, et apprehendas draconem, serpentem antiquum, qui est diabolus et satanas, ac ligatum mittas in abyssum, ut non seducat amplius gen tes. Hinc tuo confisi præsidio ac tutela, sacri ministerii nostri auctoritate [si fuerit laicus, vel clericus qui ordinem exorcistatus nondum suscepit, dicat: sacra sanctae Matris Ecclesiae auctoritate], ad infestationes diabolicæ fraudis repellendas in nomine Jesu Christi Dei et Domini nostri fidentes et securi aggredimur.

V. Ecce Crucem Domini, fugite partes adversæ.

R. Vicit Leo de tribu Juda, radix David.

V. Fiat misericordia tua, Domine, super nos.

R. Quemadmodum speravimus in te.

V. Domine, exaudi orationem meam.

R. Et clamor meus ad te veniat.

[si fuerit saltem diaconus subjungat V. Dominus vobiscum.

R. Et cum spiritu tuo.]

Oremus

Deus, et Pater Domini nostri Jesu Christi, invocamus nomen sanctum tuum, et clementiam tuam supplices exposcimus ut, per intercessionem immaculatæ semper Virginis Dei Genitricis Mariæ, beati Michaëlis Archangeli, beati Joseph ejusdem beatæ Virginis Sponsi, beatorum Apostolorum Petri et Pauli et omnium Sanctorum, adversus satanam, omnesque alios immundos spiritus, qui ad nocendum humano generi animasque perdendas pervagantur in mundo, nobis auxilium præstare digneris. Per eumdem Christum Dominum nostrum. Amen.

EXORCISMVS

Exorcizamus te, omnis immundus spiritus, omnis satanica potestas, omnis incursio infernalis adversarii, omnis legio, omnis congregatio et secta diabolica, in nomine et virtute Domini Nostri Jesu + Christi, eradicare et effugare a Dei Ecclesia, ab animabus ad imaginem Dei conditis ac pretioso divini Agni sanguine redemptis + . Non ultra audeas, serpens callidissime, decipere humanum genus, Dei Ecclesiam persequi, ac Dei electos excutere et cribrare sicut triticum + . Imperat tibi Deus altissimus + , cui in magna tua superbia te similem haberi adhuc præsumis; qui omnes homines vult salvos fieri et ad agnitionem veritaris venire. Imperat tibi Deus Pater + ; imperat tibi Deus Filius + ; imperat tibi Deus Spiritus Sanctus + . Imperat tibi majestas Christi, æternum Dei Verbum, caro factum + , qui pro salute generis nostri tua invidia perditi, humiliavit semetipsum facfus hobediens usque ad mortem; qui Ecclesiam suam ædificavit supra firmam petram, et portas inferi adversus eam nunquam esse prævalituras edixit, cum ea ipse permansurus omnibus diebus usque ad consummationem sæculi. Imperat tibi sacramentum Crucis + , omniumque christianæ fidei Mysteriorum virtus +. Imperat tibi excelsa Dei Genitrix Virgo Maria + , quæ superbissimum caput tuum a primo instanti immaculatæ suæ conceptionis in sua humilitate contrivit. Imperat tibi fides sanctorum Apostolorum Petri et Pauli, et ceterorum Apostolorum + . Imperat tibi Martyrum sanguis, ac pia Sanctorum et Sanctarum omnium intercessio +.

Ergo, draco maledicte et omnis legio diabolica, adjuramus te per Deum + vivum, per Deum + verum, per Deum + sanctum, per Deum qui sic dilexit mundum, ut Filium suum unigenitum daret, ut omnes qui credit in eum non pereat, sed habeat vitam æternam: cessa decipere humanas creaturas, eisque æternæ perditionìs venenum propinare: desine Ecclesiæ nocere, et ejus libertati laqueos injicere. Vade, satana, inventor et magister omnis fallaciæ, hostis humanæ salutis. Da locum Christo, in quo nihil invenisti de operibus tuis; da locum Ecclesiæ uni, sanctæ, catholicæ, et apostolicæ, quam Christus ipse acquisivit sanguine suo. Humiliare sub potenti manu Dei; contremisce et effuge, invocato a nobis sancto et terribili nomine Jesu, quem inferi tremunt, cui Virtutes cælorum et Potestates et Dominationes subjectæ sunt; quem Cherubim et Seraphim indefessis vocibus laudant, dicentes: Sanctus, Sanctus, Sanctus Dominus Deus Sabaoth.

V. Domine, exaudi orationem meam.

R. Et clamor meus ad te veniat.

[si fuerit saltem diaconus subjungat V. Dominus vobiscum.

R. Et cum spiritu tuo.]

Oremus.

Deus coeli, Deus terræ, Deus Angelorum, Deus Archangelorum, Deus Patriarcharum, Deus Prophetarum, Deus Apostolorum, Deus Martyrum, Deus Confessorum, Deus Virginum, Deus qui potestatem habes donare vitam post mortem, requiem post laborem; quia non est Deus præter te, nec esse potest nisi tu creator omnium visibilium et invisibilium, cujus regni non erit finis: humiliter majestati gloriæ tuæ supplicamus, ut ab omni infernalium spirituum potestate, laqueo, deceptione et nequitia nos potenter liberare, et incolumes custodire digneris. Per Christum Dominum nostrum. Amen.

Ab insidiis diaboli, libera nos, Domine.
Ut Ecclesiam tuam secura tibi facias libertate servire, te rogamus, audi nos.
Ut inimicos sanctæ Ecclesiæ humiliare digneris, te rogamus audi nos.

Et aspergatur locus aqua benedicta

Sacramentals

"AND I saw an angel come and stand before the altar, having a golden censer; and there was given to him much incense, and the smoke of the incense of the prayers of the saints ascended up before God from the hand of the angel." Revelation 8:3

The sacramentals of protection are those actions and objects which turn our hearts towards God, always remembering that He is our refuge and our hope. They acknowledge our helplessness against the snares of the devil and the lures of the world, our weakness against sin without God's help. And as they need to be, these sacramentals are very powerful. Sacramentals take various forms. Some we are all familiar are making the sign of the cross (blessing ourselves), holy water (water which has been blessed by a priest and is used, among other uses, for baptism), blessed medals and exorcisms (the blessing out of evil spirits). Sacramentals, as a rule, were not instituted by Christ (exorcism would be an obvious exception), but by the Church. Medals and crosses which have been blessed are sacramentals. If they have not been blessed, they are simply considered jewelry. The use in the Church of medals is very ancient and is intended to excite devotion and prayer. The effectiveness of a sacramental depends upon the devotion, faith and love of those who use them. Sacramentals serve to remind the faithful of the Glory of God and thereby to draw us closer to Him.

Medals

Religious medals are pieces of metal resembling coins of various sizes and shapes. They are designed to increase devotion, to commemorate some religious event, to protect the soul and body of the wearer, and to serve as a badge of membership in some society, sodality, or other spiritual group. When they are blessed, they become sacramentals.

Religious medals have been used from the dawn of Christianity. Many have been found in the catacombs, with the name of Christ and figures of the saints upon them. In the Middle Ages certain souvenirs in the form of medals were brought home as keepsakes by pilgrims to famous shrines and places of devotion.

Just like with all sacramentals, there is no "magic" benefit derived from wearing a medal, but they do prepare the wearer to receive God's grace and dispose them to cooperate with it.

Medal of Saint Benedict
(sometimes called the "Devil-chasing Medal")

One side of the medal bears an image of St. Benedict, holding a cross in the right hand and the Holy Rule in the left. On the one side of the image is a cup, on the other a raven, and above the cup and the raven are inscribed the words: "Crux Sancti Patris Benedicti" (Cross of the Holy Father Benedict). Round the margin of the medal stands the legend "Ejus in obitu nro praesentia muniamus" (May we at our death be fortified by his presence). The reverse of the medal bears a cross with the initial letters of the words: "Crux Sacra Sit Mihi Lux" (The Holy Cross be my light), written downward on the perpendicular bar; the initial letters of the words, "Non Draco Sit Mihi Dux" (Let not the dragon be my guide), on the horizontal bar; and the initial letters of "Crux Sancti Patris Benedicti" in the angles of the cross. Round the margin stand the initial letters of the distich: "Vade Retro Satana, Nunquam Suade Mihi Vana — Sunt Mala Quae Libas, Ipse Venena Bibas" (Begone, Satan, do not suggest to me thy vanities — evil are the things thou profferest, drink thou thy own poison). At the top of the cross usually stands the word

Pax (peace) or the monogram I H S(Jesus). The medal just described is the so-called jubilee medal which was struck first in 1880, to commemorate the fourteenth centenary of St. Benedict's birth. The Archabbey of Monte Cassino has the exclusive right to strike this medal The ordinary medal of St. Benedict usually differs from the preceding in the omission of the words "Ejus in obitu etc.", and in a few minor details.

Rite for Blessing Medals of Saint Benedict

Any Priest may have the faculty to bless medals of St. Benedict.

PRIEST: Our help is in the Name of the Lord.
RESPONSE: Who made heaven and earth.

PRIEST: In the Name of God, the Father + Almighty, Who made heaven and earth, the seas and all that is in them, I exorcise these medals against the power and attacks of the evil one. May all who use these medals devoutly be blessed with health of soul and body. In the Name of the Father + Almighty, of His Son + Jesus Christ our Lord, and of the Holy + Spirit, the Paraclete, and in the love of the same Lord Jesus Christ, Who will come on the last day to judge the living and the dead, and the world by fire.

RESPONSE: Amen.

PRIEST: Let us pray. Almighty God, the boundless source of all good things, we humbly ask that, through the intercession of Saint Benedict, Thou wouldst pour out Thy blessings + upon these medals. May those who use them devoutly and earnestly strive to perform good works, be blessed by Thee with health of soul and body, the grace of a holy life, a contrite spirit, and a repentant heart. May they also, with the help of Thy merciful love, resist the temptations of the evil one and strive to exercise true charity and justice toward all, so that one day they may appear sinless and holy in Thy sight. This we ask through Christ our Lord.

RESPONSE: Amen

Then the medals are sprinkled with holy water in the form of a Cross.

Salt

Since it cannot corrupt and even keeps from corruption, salt is a sign of everlasting life. One can understand how the devil hates salt, since it is an emblem of eternity and immortality. This thought is brought out in the blessing of salt for holy water. It speaks of

"salt from which the evil spirit has been cast out for the health of the faithful, and that there may be banished from the place in which thou hast been sprinkled, every kind of hallucination and wickedness, or craft of devilish deceit, and every unclean spirit."

How fittingly that holy water is used to drive out, by the

power of God, all the evil spirits. That is why you take holy water upon entering church and make with it the holy sign of the cross upon yourself. You are washing away, driving away all evil thoughts, all influence of the evil one, especially while you are adoring the Holy One in His temple. Just as that faithful man of God, Eliseus, purified the waters of the well at Jericho by putting salt into it, the priest, by blessing holy water with salt and by sprinkling it on the people as he marches down the aisle of church, drives away the devil.

Scapular of Saint Michael the Archangel

Scapulars

In the beginning, a scapular was a sort of work apron which came to symbolize the cross or yoke of Christ. They were originally shoulder-wide strips of cloth worn over the tunic and reaching almost to the ground in front and in back. By the 11th century, scapulars had become part of the habit of religious orders. Now, they are two small squares of cloth joined by strings and worn about the neck by laypersons. Scapulars are worn as a sign of association with a religious order and for devotional purposes. There have been nearly 20 different scapulars recognized by the Catholic Church, all of them are worn around the neck, either over or under other clothing. Blessing and imposition of the scapular of Saint Michael the Archangel is a practice very much feared and detested by evil spirits. This scapular takes the shape of a shield with one cord being black and the other blue. On the shield we read the words "Quis et Deus" ("I am like God"). This was Michael's reply to Lucifer, who stated "non serviam" ("I will not serve"). Michael means "Quis ut Deus" ("Who is like unto God").

Insence

Blessed Incense, like any sacramental, is most powerful when used in faith. Without faith it is useless. According to Father Gabriele Amorth, chief exorcist of Rome, whoever uses these tools with faith, obtains unhoped-for results. This Blessed Incense is very effective for homes.

It is suggested that it be burned in each room. Father Amorth also states that Incense has always been considered an antidote against evil spirits, as well as an element used to praise and adore. Liturgical use of incense remains an efficacious element of praise to God and of battle against evil. This sacramental can also mitigate the effects of the tricks that the evil one uses.

Candles

The candle has its own very beautiful meaning that came from the Old Testament practice of sacrifice. Just as the incense that sent up its cloud of perfumed smoke heavenward was a symbol of prayer, the candle consuming itself is a representation of sacrifice. The candle burnings its life out before a statue is symbolic of a person's love for God and his own desire to offer his sacrifices, and if need be, his life itself for the glory of God.

Holy Water

Holy water is a means of spiritual wealth especially when dangers threaten. The devil hates holy water because of its power over him. He cannot long tolerate a place or be near a person that is often sprinkled with this blessed water. Holy Water is water blessed by the priest for the purpose of seeking from God a blessing on those who use it and protection from the powers of darkness. Holy water is used for baptism and rites of blessing and purification. Holy Water sanctifies whoever is touched by it, frees him from uncleanness and attacks of the powers of darkness, and secures that wherever it is sprinkled there is freedom from pestilence and snares of Satan.

St. Theresa of Avila on holy water: "From long experience I have learned that there is nothing like holy water to put devils to flight and prevent them from coming back again. They also flee from the cross, but return; so holy water must have great value."

BLESSED OLIVE OIL

The use of blessed Olive Oil is particularly effective, because it contains the prayer of exorcism at the very beginning. "Exorcizo te, creatura olei" ("I exorcise, creature oil"). "Omis virtus adversarii, omnis exceritus diaboli, omnis incúrus, omne phatasma Satanæ eradicare" ("All power of the adversary, all diabolical armies, all hostile attack, eliminating every satanic apparition"). "Uf fiat ómnibus, qui eo usuri sunt, salus menti et corporis" ("and all who would use this would have health of mind and body"). Further into the prayer, it states that all those who are sick would be free of "Ab omni languore" ("all weakness, languor, listlessness"), "omni qui infirmitate" ("all sickness") and "insidiis inimici liberéntur", ("freed of any snares of the enemy"). And "cunctae adversitates separéntur a pusmate tuo" (all of the opposing powers that separate your creature from you).

Made in the USA
Lexington, KY
15 January 2010